WHEN THE EARTH TREMBLED!

WHEN
The EARTH
TREMBLED!

MEMORIALS, TESTIMONIES, AND SPIRITUAL LESSONS

JEAN JOREL CLAUDE

Xulon Press

Xulon Press
2301 Lucien Way #415
Maitland, FL 32751
407.339.4217
www.xulonpress.com

Edited by Xulon Press.

Printed in the United States of America.

ISBN-13: 9781545626856

Foreword

"It is often said that the character of a man is the result of what he has lived through and the people he has been with" (Unknown).

This book tells the story of one of the worst disasters of our generation narrated by an exceptional individual who, by choice, lived several months with his family in a tent while caring for a community of more than one hundred people.

In January 2010, I found myself in Port-au-Prince four days after the earthquake that killed several hundred thousand people and caused more than one million people to be homeless. I was accompanied by a team of rescuers from the United States and the Dominican Republic. Since all communications were suspended the day after the disaster, we faced a major challenge in planning our mission.

However, we left with the faith that God, who called us to help our brothers and sisters in Haiti, would guide us.

On the ground, Jean-Jorel Claude, a longtime friend, was responsible for an important congregation. While all the victims of the earthquake were busy making an assessment of material and humans in their own surrounding, Jorel was dealing with the helplessness of several hundred people under his care, all impacted by the disaster. The enormous and complex work in front of him included the organization of health care for the injured, the search for missing relatives, food preparation, and arrangement of a housing shelter (because several members of the congregation had lost their homes).

Driven by his love for God's people under his charge, Jorel demonstrated courage, creativity, compassion, and unequaled resourcefulness.

In the pages that follow, he gives us his perspective and the lessons that he learned, as well, from this painful and transformative episode of his life.

Let yourself be inspired by his personal, simple, and honest narrative.

Stanley Dumornay

Contents

ACKNOWLEDGMENTS AND DEDICATION

I would first of all like to thank God for having guided me to finish this book. I am filled with joy and gratitude to have discovered a deep taste for such a gratifying activity. However, I would not have realized it if Junie my wife had not encouraged me to do it. That is why I want to thank her wholeheartedly by dedicating this book to her, which I hope she will read with pleasure. I also dedicate this book to Jova and Elie, my two boys, who, throughout the work, have not stopped asking me this question: Papi, when are you going to finish this book?

I would also like to dedicate this book to Mollie Mostert for the impact that she has had on the refugees in the camp, on my wife, and on me particularly, at the relief shelter of Canapé-Vert.

My thanks also go to you all, my brothers, who contributed by your encouragement to the outcome of this project. Some gave me wholesome advice. Others supplied me the photos they had in their archives. And still others have voluntarily produced written testimonies in order to support this initiative. I couldn't forget those who have sacrificed long hours of their precious time to do a critical reading of the manuscript.

I thank my niece, Vanessa Celestin, for her help in finalizing the work. I appreciate the work done by Sanders Joseph. Thank you, Sandy!

I can't forget Margalie Viélot. She accomplished one of the most complicated tasks of the book—the translation. From the French version, the book can be read now in English as well under her skillful work. Thank you so much for your patience, my sister.

Special thanks go to Stanley Dumornay and André Paul Vénor for their unwavering support.

Finally, for the cooperation received to accomplish this novel, saying thank you doesn't represent much.

I sign this book, but the credit comes back to many people.

JJC

Preamble

Why another book on the earthquake?

The earthquake that struck Haiti in 2010 was among the events that have left an indelible and painful mark on the history of the Haitian people. Many professional writers have devoted much ink to this subject, authors such as Yanick Lahens in her essay "Breaches," and Marc Perrault who wrote *Under the Rubbles of the Montana Hotel,* just to name a few. But, as one of the people who were there at the time of the earthquake and having seen and learned many things that have opened my eyes, it seemed fitting for me to write a book as well: *When the Earth Trembled,* with the goal of presenting a balanced account, where the emphasis would be placed more on the spiritual dimension of this human tragedy.

To achieve this project, the history of the country was reviewed loosely, and some parts have been kept as contributing arguments. To this will be added references to some reports produced by international agencies and humanitarian organizations deployed to Haiti at the time of the earthquake.

Those who survived this cataclysm, those who were there in the core of the drama, should take a moment of silence and think.

The objective would be to attempt to make sense of why they were spared while thousands of others had fallen and to live each day for this reason.

However, this book is not intended only as a reflection for Haitians. The misfortune of the Haitian people is to a certain extent mankind's misfortune, and the lessons to be learned are valid for all. Proof of that includes the efforts that have already been made by an outpouring of mixed solidarity (Haitians and foreigners alike) to pull the country from the slump the day after January 12, 2010. Haiti was not alone. Two or three days after the drama, just a few meters from the Haiti Church of Christ's property, we heard gunshots under the rubble of a collapsed building. This apartment block was predominantly inhabited by soldiers of the UN security mission deployed on the ground since 2004 at the time of the political crisis post-Aristide. Stuck way at the bottom of the underground garage of the building under tons of concrete, these soldiers were shooting to signal that they were still alive and desperately needed help. The Dominicans were the first to arrive and then were later joined by other international first aid workers. They displayed a whole arsenal of equipment to lend the strong hand to the rescue of these men in danger because they were better equipped. They did not entirely succeed, but they were there fighting beside the Haitians to save those who could still be saved.

Globalization has transformed the modern world into one big village and every country into a small district. It is what justifies all the initiatives undertaken by the international community to improve the lot of the victims and to support the reconstruction of Haiti.

And since then:

- So many big meetings for this cause were convened!

- So many promising speeches were made!

- And a lot of money was collected!

From the smallest to the greatest, from the simple citizen to the largest organizations, in schools as in hospitals, people from everywhere gave to help Haiti with its overwhelming needs.

In this same vein, author Dany Laferrière writes in his book *Everything Moves around Me*:

It is in the streets of Montreal that I was able to review the immense emotion that the misfortune of Haiti caused. People seem affected in the depths of themselves. It seems like the city only vibrates for Haiti. I come home to see on TV all these heartbroken faces (still in close-up). Nurses scrambling to go treat the wounded, children collecting money by all means (by selling sketches or by organizing small shows) which they would give to humanitarian bodies, amateur and professional musicians who send the total taking of their shows to orphanages, suburban rockers with their Mohawk haircut wearing T-shirts with I love Haiti printed on it, reporters who want to adopt children whom they would take in their arms for the sake of a report, huge concerts like in the time of "We are the World," which yield several millions of dollars in one night, stars of Hollywood who sell their gala dresses to be able to send food, stars who use their private planes to transport medicine, doctors who operate until exhaustion, not to mention the anonymous crowd who wants to work with modesty and discretion. But where goes all this energy? Where does all this money go? We want to help so much that we don't try to know. The sadness on their faces alternates with the will to really do something, and to do it personally. Haiti has just entered their intimacy with such a crash. [1]

This observation made in Montreal by Laferrière was only a sample of all the activities carried out in several corners of the planet with the same enthusiasm and the same objective. We can all agree that many resources throughout the whole world had been mobilized to give a proportional answer to the big challenges that the collapsed country faced. The momentum was well underway and felt by more than one. Certain Haitians, even eternally pessimistic to the real development of the country, witnessed the great dialogue that emerged around this humanitarian crisis. The consultation, which included a series of leading figures of the political world along with international showbiz, showed that even these disbelievers had come to believe that the knell for poverty of Haiti had finally sounded. An opportunity offered on a silver platter had finally come for the country to find its path toward development.

But what finally happened?

One does not need to have a degree in social sciences to realize that expectations are still not fulfilled. Eight years later, there are still people who live in tents in Port-au-Prince. At the same time, as I draft this very paragraph, sixty-five Haitian gourdes are the equivalent of one US dollar. The first night, the price of the basic goods soared. Masses of people passing under wires continue to search underground for work in spite of the ill treatment imposed by Dominican immigration policies to discourage those who would eventually want to cross. Many of my fellow countrymen have begun to fly away toward Brazil or Chile, with the intuition that something better awaits them there under the heavens of South America. All these indications bring to light how much the socioeconomic situation of the Haitian people has seriously been degraded. It is obvious that the projects realized during these first eight years since the crisis are far from corresponding to the promises uttered after the disaster.

Why?

Because, in its nature, the real problem of Haiti is deeper than what holds our attention. The earthquake must be perceived as an alarm, activated by God to attract the attention of our people to him, to learn to place our ranging-poles on the right side.

Today, more than political or socioeconomic, the real problem of Haiti is rather a spiritual order as seen in chapter four of Amos.

This is why this book is written, not only by way of testimony, but especially so that other solutions can be put in perspective — solutions that money and government programs cannot replace. And that our hope is thus directed to surer promises, those that do not come from men but from God.

My prayer is that this book can be useful to you.

Happy reading and may God bless you!

Plan of the Book

This book is divided into eight chapters. Each chapter focuses either on a specific subject symbolizing one of the phases of the earthquake or representing a situation experienced at the campsite on the property of our church in Canapé-Vert. It was there that I found shelter for hundreds of days with my family, together with other traumatized members from the congregation. For the tragic character of the narrative, it is considered wiser to adopt this approach, with the aim of allowing the reader to live the story in fragments while allowing for a global view of what had exactly happened.

Spiritual lessons along with relevant biblical passages have been extracted for the edification of the reader. Because it is obvious that after a while, certain Scriptures seem to lose their initial meaning by modernization and the scientific progress. They seem to be unrealistic and even utopian. For example, let us consider this verse: "But if we have food and clothing, we will be content with that" (1Timothy 6:8). How do you understand this verse in a world where materialism has dominated?

However, we had a good answer to this question in the morning of January 13, 2010, although it was in a way that we would never have wished. Indeed, several thousands of Haitians began that day, from being wealthy the previous day to finding themselves in total poverty. And that morning, far from thinking of luxury, the survivors were rather focused on the bare minimum of food and clothing in order to survive, not the things that they had lost. In the camp of Canapé-Vert, we had to learn to live the first days of the crisis with just these two things. I admit that it was painful for people as sophisticated as us, who had been accustomed to comfort. But, it was necessary to go through that to understand how this scripture is not just an ideal tied to simplicity, but rather a situation that anyone can come up against right in the middle of the twenty-first century. At least, that is what this crisis showed. Thus to comprehend this scripture in depth, the reality of the disaster brought real meaning for several of us of whom I was the first. Its application was very tangible in the life of many in Haiti, starting with ours in the camp of Canapé-Vert.

Henceforth, we understood that the blessings that God gives us besides food and clothing should not be taken for granted. On the contrary, they should be used to please the Lord while developing a real appreciation for them.

Note: The same method of work was adopted for every chapter with different passages while considering the relevant matter.

The references have been provided for further reading.

Pleasant reading!

CHAPTER 1

THE PREPARATION

THE PREPARATION

Events happen sometimes when you least expect them.

It was a normal day, a peaceful one in Haiti, that Tuesday of January 12, 2010. It was filled with all the freshness of the New Year. In the morning, when we woke up, the weather was very clear. Already, we could see the first beams of the sun faithful to its appointments. Everything was going peacefully. The usual activities were going at full capacity. Nothing of the national life had been impaired in any way. Because the political climate had been relatively favorable, it was easy to notice the serene atmosphere throughout the streets of Port-au-Prince. Tap-taps (type of public transportation in Haiti) as usual assured the public mobility. Private and public offices offered their services to the population, and schools had opened their doors to offer the bread of instructions to the students. Thus nothing, absolutely nothing, was suggesting that the earthquake was going to occur that same afternoon. There was no evidence during that day, or even the days of the previous week. The minds were rather focused on making new resolutions for the new year of 2010. In a nutshell, we can say that no day could have been more beautiful and more active than that of that Tuesday of January 12.

It wasn't until late afternoon that that bright day was going to turn into darkness, to everyone's surprise. Effectively, it was 4:50 pm, when on the Richter scale, an earthquake of magnitude 7.0 suddenly occurred in Haiti. It is classified by the experts among the deadliest natural disasters of modern history, leaving behind according to the official sources, an unparalleled record:

- 230,000–300,000 deaths.

- 300,572 wounded persons.

- 1.3 million homeless persons. [2]

These are figures that Haiti will take a while to forget because the impact was big and the emotional pain so severe.

Better Safe than Sorry

Si m te konen toujou dèyè.

This is a commonly used Haitian proverb which means: "I would have done it differently if I had known beforehand"

It is that expression that comes to mind when we miss an opportunity to do something good. Or also, when we made a mistake that leads to annoying consequences. We would have liked to be able to follow the theory of "the butterfly effect" (Evan Treborn), to go back if it was possible, to repair these errors, and avoid the consequences. But unfortunately, the laws of nature do not, in most circumstances, open doors to such possibilities. Otherwise, how many scenes would we have canceled from the movie? How many pages would we have eliminated from the book? But, "No one is bound to do what is impossible" says Charles Nisard.[3] Then the best that we can do now is to learn from these mistakes—without being able to erase or being enslaved by them—to become better for the next movie or book of our human life.

From the Event of the Earthquake, What Can We Learn?

Tap-Tap

The first big lesson is to train to be ready. The parable of the ten virgins illustrates very well the essential elements for a good preparation. It is to take information seriously and to act with diligence. It says:

> At that time the kingdom of heaven will be like ten virgins who took their lamps and went out to meet the bridegroom.

> Five of them were foolish and five were wise.

> The foolish ones took their lamps but did not take any oil with them. The wise ones, however, took oil in jars along with their lamps.

> The bridegroom was a long time in coming, and they all became drowsy and fell asleep. At midnight the cry rang out: "Here's the bridegroom! Come out to meet him!"

Then all the virgins woke up and trimmed their lamps. The foolish ones said to the wise, "Give us some of your oil; our lamps are going out."

"No," they replied, "there may not be enough for both us and you. Instead, go to those who sell oil and buy some for yourselves."

But while they were on their way to buy the oil, the bridegroom arrived. The virgins who were ready went in with him to the wedding banquet. And the door was shut.

Later the others also came. "Lord, Lord," they said, "open the door for us!" But he replied, "Truly I tell you, I don't know you."

Therefore keep watch, because you do not know the day or the hour. (Matthew 25:1–13)

It is obvious that the ten virgins were aware of the imminent arrival of the bridegroom. Consequently, from this information, you can see them waiting for him, which was very commendable on their part. On the other hand, we realize that they were all exhausted and were sleepy while waiting. They all had the same opportunities while facing the same challenges. We have to understand that all the virgins were placed at the same level. However, at one point a seemingly insignificant but serious decision divides them in two subgroups: the wise and the foolish.

Why?

The whole difference resides in the simple fact that the wise ones took extra oil with them. They obtained what was required to be able to keep the fire on their lamps burning when it was time. The foolish ones, however, failed to take extra of the precious liquid when they took their lamps.

The Consequences

When the bridegroom arrived is when the pressure increased. The foolish ones panicked, wanting to pull all the stops. They first turned toward the other virgins (the wise) to get help. But, unfortunately, they could not meet their need. They were encouraged to go buy from those who sell. But it was too late because when they came back to the house, the door was already closed.

As a result, they missed the opportunity to meet the bridegroom by the simple fact that the oil ran out in their lamps. They were unable to keep it lit.

Whereas, for the wise, it was a party. They were able to meet the bridegroom easily and remain inside with him.

To Learn

1. The Nontransferable Values

There are values that cannot be passed on to others. They are not transferable as donations. Each virgin had to have her own oil for her own lamp. For example, a parent cannot one morning say to his child, "My son or my daughter, you know that I love you very much. I am old, and today I would like to pass on to you my faith in God." Or reversely, the child who becomes an adult believes that he has inherited the faith of his parents. That's not how it works. The parents can inspire their children by their examples of faith, they can pray for them, point them in the right direction, or even train them so that they can build it; but they won't be able to transplant their own faith to their children. We're talking about a long-term exercise. And sometimes, even though we do all we can as parents to engage our children, it is not automatically guaranteed that they are going to become like us—men or women of faith. It is merely our part of the intricate process of transformation of their heart, of which God is the only craftsman. However, in sowing and watering, we point our children in a good position to embark naturally when they will be visited by God.

That is what Paul said in 1 Corinthians 3:6: *I planted the seed, and Apollos watered it, but God has been making it grow.*

Anything else can be bequeathed with a duly signed document. But, not our faith.

It is because each has his own lamp with its own oil. It simply means that we each must develop our own faith to have access to the grace offered freely by God and get our own convictions to remain faithful until the end. And we are not to rely on both the faith and the convictions of others.

2. The Risk of Going to Look Somewhere Else

The term risk is mentioned because they (the foolish) dared to leave the house, where the bridegroom was supposed to meet them. Crossing the threshold away from where the bridegroom would be—if only for a short time and even for the oil that we believe we need—may be a risk of eternal significance because when they came back, the door was already closed. Hence, it's understandable when we don't do what must be done, and within the time limit set, it is possible to miss some golden opportunities that would not be found again, even though we would be willing to pay a fortune to make up for lost time. The neglected things of today, if proven to be important, will mark us sometimes for a whole life, depending upon its level of significance.

All it takes is just a little carelessness, along with a few minutes of sleep, to tilt everything to the wrong side, with serious damages.

What Is the Best Option in All That?

The best option would be to imitate the wise virgins. By definition *"to get ready"* means to do everything possible to be ready when the time comes, to succeed (Larousse).

From this definition it is easy to understand why the wise virgins had succeeded and the foolish ones had failed. It was a matter of attitude.

> When we don't do what must be done, and within the time limit set; it is possible to miss some golden opportunities that would not be found again, even though we would be willing to pay a fortune to make up for lost time.

The wise ones had the attitude that was necessary. They showed alertness, foresight, and seriousness. That is why, justifiably, their efforts were crowned with success.

The Weakness of the Foolish Virgins

The foolish virgins, in turn, didn't have the kind of attitude that was necessary. For such a special appointment, there was obviously a lack of anticipation on their part. They did not think about what they would need in the long run and to prepare themselves accordingly. At the end of the day, you see them waiting for an appointment for which they were not ready. That is why their efforts resulted in failure.

Therefore, the point in all this is that we must strive to imitate the wise virgins. There is a Haitian saying that goes *ranje kabann ou anvan domi nan je w* that literally means "Turn down your bed before you get sleepy." It implies to fight a daily battle against laziness, complacency, thoughtlessness, and especially against procrastination because without realizing it, these are the character flaws that weigh people down and drive them to various setbacks all their lives, from the most humble to the highest decision makers.

Applicable in All Areas of Daily Life

Allow me to tell you that this is valid for all areas of daily life. For example, in the beginning of this chapter, the word *suddenly* was mentioned to describe the character unexpected of the earthquake of 2010 by the Haitians. But actually, it was the day and the hour that were sudden and not the earthquake itself because it has been anticipated and had been predicted. In fact, at least two or three years before the dawning of the seism, the engineer Claude Prépetit had not failed to ring the alert signal in the news. In his booklet titled *Hazard and Seismic Risk in Haiti,* he presented an ongoing basis how likely the risk was to have a temblor in Haiti. To repeat in his own words, he wrote:

We cannot stop an earthquake from occurring in Haiti; because, it is a natural phenomenon. On the other hand, based on the data provided by the studies made about this, we can limit the losses; mitigate the effects by reducing the vulnerability of the population. [4]

This engineer had become famous for having so often alerted the national opinion on the potential threat that we faced. One day, he was interviewed in one of the most popular radio programs in the country, and the reporter asked him the following question: "Engineer, have you no fear of being labeled the inauspicious prophet, by constantly predicting the imminence of such a disaster on the country?" I don't remember his answer. But the nature of the question leads to conclude that it was consistent in the popularization of his message.

Therefore, the state authorities had been warned. The population of the big cities, in particular that of Port-au-Prince, had heard about it. It is a shame that his message was preached in the desert. The scientific explanations provided by the engineer on the possibility of an earthquake, with the express purpose of compelling the people to take action were not taken seriously — until the cataclysm happened and caused so much devastation. Eight years later, the burden of the aftermath is still very heavy in the life of the Haitian people. And only God knows when the day of relief will be for the citizens of the island to have access to a better life.

To Retain

What should be learned, even if everything else is forgotten, is that there will always be natural disasters that will hit one place or another on our planet.

During the last trimester of 2016 only, certain places were struck like Haiti was: destruction by the Hurricane Matthew in both the South and Grand-Anse departments, Italy by an earthquake of 6.5 on the Richter scale, and New Zealand by a seism of 7.8 on the same scale. Take a look also on what happened in Puerto Rico in September 2017. How it was completely destroyed by the devastating Hurricane Maria.

What country is next? And with what type of natural disaster?

So, it is clear, there is nothing we can do to protect our countries against natural phenomenon. And in that domain, all barriers have come down. Whether we are dealing with countries in the developed or the third world, the nations from the North or the South, rich or impoverished areas, we are unable to keep ourselves from being hit when nature unleashes itself. It is just out of any human control. However, with careful preparation and well-calculated preventive measures, we can reduce the losses and soften the blow.

Relevant Also in Our Individual Lives

This logic is just as relevant in our individual lives. We cannot live and be exempt of situations that the average person faces. For example, to get married and have children afterward are events naturally recorded in the normal cycle of the human life since the beginning of time. And, at this very hour, there are thousands of marriages being performed around the world, and thousands of new spouses being added to the big parental family in adding a new member to their progeny.

But, if the newlyweds, happy today of their new experience, were not prepared mentally and spiritually for what awaits them tomorrow in their home, this blessing could turn into a disaster, when the passion of the honeymoon and the romance of the first weeks wear off. I am referring to the one that we use to read about in the books, such as "Rodrigue and Chimène" of Corneille, or "Romeo and Juliet" of Shakespeare, for example. Neither is it the kind of couples that we refer to in reading volumes of romance novels. All of a sudden we leave the unrealistic phase of the marriage behind to face the reality of living with someone else. This is exactly where the challenge for a successful marriage begins. The choice is then offered to the new couple: either to build together or to fight, depending on whether they were prepared or not at the signing of the covenant of marriage in the presence of witnesses. Evidently, it would always have been more desirable that they lean toward the first option, that of unity to build their future, than to get into endless conflicts. But they must be prepared or begin to get ready. After all, it is never too late once we have a heart ready to learn.

The Same Pattern for Parents

This principle of preparedness is also valid for new parents. Nothing can be more exciting than to see your offspring. It is a celebration in the home; you receive many visitors, presents for the baby, and congratulatory cards for you. Everybody is happy, looking at the infant lying in their crib with their eyes closed and their little fists clenched. Friends tell you, "Wow! How cute they are!"

We are at that point filled with a feeling of exhilaration and unsuspected sense of pride as parents. But watch out! Do you know that children, cute today, who bring you so much pride, can become a thorn in the flesh tomorrow if you are not ready to be there for them in their lives until they grow up? A parent should be prepared to support their children, especially in the critical phase of their teenage years. It does not amount to offering expensive toys to the children and to provide them with all that they need materially, without being active in their lives. All parameters of life can change in the existence of children while growing up: their toys or their clothes, their schools or their home town, but the presence of a parent should never be substituted for anything in the world unless it is absolutely necessary and cannot be helped. This is the best present a responsible parent should offer to oneself and their children, to be active in their lives and to spend quality time that will leave in them a permanent mark that will be extremely positive on their character.

Conclusion

Man cannot avoid being tested. However, getting ready to face the hardships—especially when we know that they are inevitable—is the expression that should resonate strongly at the bottom of our soul.

Why?

Because the earthquake is not only the disaster that breaks the buildings and

> The earthquake is not only the disaster that breaks the buildings and makes the ground dance under our feet, it is also the one that, at another level, plunders with violence the foundation of our community: marriages, families, and the youth. It is the one that, emotionally and spiritually, still causes more damages and deaths every day than was made physically by that of January 12, 2010, in Haiti.

makes the ground dance under our feet, it is also the one that, at another level, plunders with violence the foundation of our community: marriages, families, and the youth. It is the one that, emotionally and spiritually, still causes more damages and deaths every day than was made physically by that of January 12, 2010, in Haiti. Therefore, whatever platform you want to consider, we don't have any choice other than to adopt the sovereign attitude to face the uncertainties of the future both in our countries as well as in our lives. It is the attitude that consists in building well, starting today, in preparation of what will come tomorrow.

CHAPTER 2

SOLID WITHOUT CEMENT

SOLID WITHOUT CEMENT

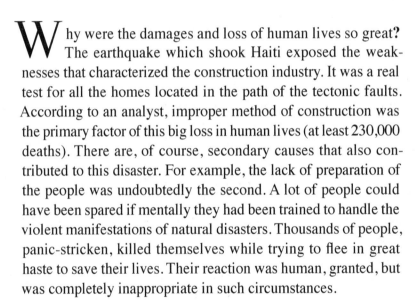

W hy were the damages and loss of human lives so great? The earthquake which shook Haiti exposed the weaknesses that characterized the construction industry. It was a real test for all the homes located in the path of the tectonic faults. According to an analyst, improper method of construction was the primary factor of this big loss in human lives (at least 230,000 deaths). There are, of course, secondary causes that also contributed to this disaster. For example, the lack of preparation of the people was undoubtedly the second. A lot of people could have been spared if mentally they had been trained to handle the violent manifestations of natural disasters. Thousands of people, panic-stricken, killed themselves while trying to flee in great haste to save their lives. Their reaction was human, granted, but was completely inappropriate in such circumstances.

Historic Jump

In short, we need to take a leap in the history of Haiti to better understand why and how the style of building in the country, and particularly in Port-au-Prince, would be put on trial for being the primary factor responsible for the death of most of the people on January 12, 2010.

The Rural Migration

Everything started with the rural migration. In 1957, Doctor François Duvalier, also known as Papa Doc was elected president of the Republic of Haiti. Very early, he began a propaganda campaign that consisted of bringing into the capital many people from all the geographical departments of the country for the celebration of the day of sovereignty and national recognition (September 22). It also marked the date of his election to the primary judiciary of the country. We would learn later that there was something fishy going on in the setting of this propaganda machine. His motive was purely political because he wanted to show the world just how popular he was in the country in order to later justify the presidency for life that he was strongly coveting. He would therefore repeat the same thing every year during all the duration of his tenure. Trucks would be sent to the various provinces to bring a large audience to his speech, which was traditionally held on the ground of the national palace on the specified date.

Were They Compelled to Respond to This Invitation?

This marked the beginning of the rural migration toward the capital that is still going on to this day. At that time, the dictatorship was so fierce that any type of resistance could mean death; therefore, the people did not have the choice of turning down the invitation, better yet the summons, of the president. So, they would fill up the trucks sent for them and go to Port-au-Prince to cheer and applaud the head of state on the ground of the national palace shouting, *"Vive, Papa Doc"*!

Another thing to consider is the fact that at that time, Port-au-Prince was the beacon city that a vast majority of Haitians dreamed of visiting. This event created a big temptation for a rural citizen to whom a free trip to the capital was offered. We could even say that this trip to the palace was like a promotion for the self-esteem of the peasant.

Also, according to what the short history discloses, transportation for these people was only provided for the trip to Port-au-Prince and not for the way back. This presumed that it was only the ones who were willing and were able to pay for the trip back and had solid ties in their village who would go back to their hometown. It offered the perfect excuse for the others to stay, especially if they had always had that dream. As a result, they were easily added among the residents of Port-au-Prince, and most of the time with the collusion of friends and other relatives already settled in the city.

A Second Explanation for the Migration

In the 1970s, some new factories opened their door in the outsourcing industry, creating new jobs in the city of Port-au-Prince. At that same time, the farming industry was struggling. The workforce that depended the farming industry was more and more diminished. So far, no attempt was made to improve local production. The tools used were still very basic. Most irrigation conduits, because of their lack of upkeep, were unable to deliver the water to the plantations. As a result, the crops were well below the projected average and were not proportional to the work and investment made by the peasants whose livelihood depended on it. Then, drawn by the prospect of finding a job in the factories in the capital, they came en masse in search of something better, particularly since working in a factory at minimum wage brought more income than working on the farm and was less tiresome.

A Third Explanation for the Migration

The third reason for the migration was the fact that Port-au-Prince was seen by the majority of Haitians as the city of luck. And with good reason because most of the public services were available only in the region of the capital. For example, to obtain a passport, or even go to university after the end of secondary school, you had to travel to the city. Thus, very little was planned in the rural regions to retain the people in their hometown by making available to them all that a human being aspires to naturally. This led to an unrivalled migratory movement over the years with a remarkable increase at the time of the embargo imposed on Haiti by the international community in the 1990s.

Let us see the evolution of the population of Port-au-Prince during the last three decades before the earthquake. According to The Haitian Institute of Statistics and Data Processing (HISDP), we have the following figures.

Year	POPULATION
1980	715,949
1990	1,141,000
1996	1,500,000
2010	4,000,000

By considering the thirty years that preceded the earthquake, we can observe a Port-au-Prince swamped by the migratory flow. The city had transformed into a true capital of problems. The existing infrastructures were no longer suitable to meet the needs of this high population growth and had not been expanded to accommodate the needs of the population. And this started the phenomenon of the uncontrolled construction to alleviate a crucial need for housing.

The Newcomers and the Housing

They formed two groups: the fortunate and the less fortunate. The first ones were those who had a connection with people already settled in the city (friends or family). They were able to live with those people for a while.

The less fortunate, those who stayed in the city after the festivity of September 22 with no money and having no one to turn to, had no other choice but to take refuge in trucks parked at the stations of the capital to spend the night or to lie down in front of the stores downtown. But how long were they able to live like this? Another Haitian proverb goes like this: "*tout bèt jennen mòde*." which means "any strained animal will bite." Thus, the difficult situation in which the peasants found themselves in terms of housing prompted them to want to own their own little home. And from then on, they began to do everything in their power to build themselves a house.

The big question: how were they going to proceed to build their homes?

I am not a technician in this field, but I understood from talking to friends who are architects and engineers that there are some factors that could place a house in the batch of poor construction and that a builder should take into consideration.

The Factor of the Quality of the Materials

The people who came from the provinces as part of the rural migration lacked everything. It must be understood that they had left their hometown in search of something better. To survive in the capital, they would do small jobs like push wheelbarrows to transport goods or wash cars at various corners of the capital, and the women themselves became small retailers or maids, which they are still doing today. In this way, they were able to earn some money to buy themselves worn-out clothes (commonly called *pèpè*) in the booth of Croix des Bossales (area designated for the sale of second-hand goods), and to eat a plate of *chen jambe* (Haitian jargon to describe a cheap plate of food cooked at a street corner), and the rest of their income was earmarked for the construction of the house. This paints the picture of the life of the least fortunate of the migrants.

But the more fortunate, because of the benefit of having people already settled in the city, were able to find a job in the out-sourcing industry or in the stores or even in the public or private administration. Let me point out that although the latter had rel-atively a much better salary and had a more decent standard of living, they were still unable to build a house that met the stan-dards. And as their financial capacity was far from being able to enable them to buy themselves quality materials, they reverted to go to the black market (Marche Salomon, for example) to embark on making their dream a reality. Many houses built in Haiti were done by the acquisition of second-hand materials (sheet metal, wood, toilet, door, window panes, etc.).

BAD CONSTRUCTION, MADE ESSENTIALLY OF
SALVAGED MATERIALS

The Factor of the Quality of the Land

When we think about the quality of the land, there are three aspects to consider.

The Legality of the Land

During Duvalier's reign (1957–1986), a lot of Haitian citizens left the country voluntarily to avoid the dictatorial regime that was raging at the time. Still others were exiled by the government because of their political beliefs. [5] In most cases, those people, when they migrated to other countries, left behind important real estate, including empty lots. The context of the fall of Duvalier's son (Baby Doc) in 1986 opened the floodgate of the invasion of free domains, whether private or public, to those who were waiting for an opportunity like this to implement their project to plant their four posts, as they like to say. This phenomenon will help us understand why there are so many illegal land occupants in Haiti. They don't have the authentic titles for the property where they live. Another Haitian proverb tells us: "*Chodyè prete pa bouyi pwa sèch*" which literally means that a borrowed pot won't cook dry beans.

What application can we make of this proverb in the context of the land occupants who are not real owners?

The point is that these people know very well that at any time they can legally be asked to vacate the place for not having the legal deed of the property. They understand that they are there temporarily; therefore, they don't want to make any big investments to build themselves strong houses, aside from the fact that they did not have too much money.

You should not, however, generalize these facts. Citizens who are conscientious did not take this illegal option and preferred to lease a plot of land—no matter how small—to build their houses, instead of getting a hold of a portion that did not rightfully belong to them.

The Type of Soil

All land does not have the same geophysical makeup. Some is suited for farming, some is clay-like, and still other land is sandy. The list goes on and on about what would make a land unsuited for construction. In that sense, the lands should be surveyed so that the geotechnical engineer can be sure that the land is suitable for construction. It is necessary to establish zoning. Otherwise, the land must be conditioned to be used for construction at an additional cost to the initial budget. When these actions are not taken in advance, the investment made in the construction of the small or large buildings is not guaranteed.

The Location of the Land

There are regions where all forms of construction are forbidden as part of the zoning.

Below is incidentally what the National Building Code of Haiti, released in 2012, stated about high-risk areas:

Article 1.4.2.1

The following high-risk zones must be avoided:

a—50 m on all sides of the precise layout of an active hole.

b—The gullies and steep slopes (more than 36% or 20 degree angle) c—Landslide areas or shaky slopes of which the shifts can be caused by an earthquake or strong rains.

d—Shaky lands, movable ground, the liquefiable soils, soft clays, swampy areas or mangrove, region of aggradations.

e—Brownfield lands (garbage dumps, building scraps).

f—Flood-prone areas (50 m from the seaside, less than 25 m from the gullies, or less than 10 m from the side of unenclosed gullies).

g—The lowest parts of the ocean coasts susceptible to be affected by tsunamis.

h—Termite-infested zones.

When we build in these restricted areas despite the prohibitions of the legal requirements, it undoubtedly culminates in a public health hazard.

The Factor of the Technicality of the Construction

Construction is an important industry that requires know-how from the builders. Only individuals who are trained and master the science and the techniques of this art should work in this field. The temptation is very strong in Haiti not to hire an engineer to implement building projects aside from, of course, wealthy people, global corporations, and a fringe of the middle class. There are many who prefer to consult a *"bos mason"* or a foreman to build their house. In no time, the walls are up by adding a little visual appeal, with no regard for the technical aspect of the work. The owners think that they can use the money they would have paid the engineer to get more done. The thing is, a house can be beautiful enough to draw attention and to bring some praise to its owner and its builder while being a real danger for the occupants because it simply doesn't meet the technical and scientific building standards.

An example that had touched my heart comes from the engineer who was overseeing the construction of my own house. As part of his work, he had to travel to the South for one week. Before leaving, he gave specific instructions to the foreman on the technique to use to make an archway. When he came back, while checking, he saw that part of the work was not well done. I watched the two men arguing for a few minutes holding the floor plan of the house. And finally, the engineer asked the foreman to tear down the bad part of the bricklaying and to do it over. Since this happened in front of me, I said to myself "*My God.*" It was like someone had dropped a pot of frozen water on me, when I heard that the engineer had decided that the work had to be redone.

I was anxious, after two years of waiting to move in. I was looking forward to enjoying again this familial atmosphere—our little pad—that we had before the disaster. Because of it, I counted every working day, and my patience in every stop was tested. Then, I took the engineer to the side to convince him to have a change of mind because in my opinion he had no grounds for getting to this point and because I wanted to see the work moving, avoiding the additional expenses and so anticipate my final dream. This is when he taught me about specific techniques, which cannot be frivolously treated. He made me understand that the house did not belong to me until he handed me the key at the end of the operation. I must confess that my relationship with this engineer did not begin with the construction of the house. Not only were we brothers in Christ, but he was also someone with whom I had a tight, friendly relationship for years.

Thus, when he declined my request, with an argument so frank and direct, I understood that he was really serious about the application of the principles of his profession, rather than to compromise to please a friend. I believe that it is a good example of the respect for standards; it is also what makes all the difference in the resistance of a house in the face of disasters. I believe that the story of the house of my father-in-law is also a very convincing example, and I promise to speak about it later. But when the technical aspect is compromised during the erection of a building, we have to expect unpleasant surprises when the times of crisis come.

The Factor of Poor Maintenance

Another reason that must be added to the list of the causes that led to the collapse of such a large number of houses is poor maintenance. A lot of the oldest houses, especially those that were not well maintained over the years, bent easily under the jolts of the earthquake, particularly if they were built in the trajectory of the tectonic faults. It must be stressed, to be honest, that we Haitians have no culture of maintenance. We have a different mentality about what we build—that the roads, bridges, and buildings will last forever. It doesn't take too long for our infrastructural realizations to be shelved until a misfortune comes and forces us to adopt the fireman's attitude. Such was the fate of many public or private collapsed buildings. With time, their foundations became rotten, and when there is no foundation, the structure is not livable, even if the framework remains standing.

The Factor of the Irresponsibility of the Authorized Agents

You have just obtained an overview of the various reasons that led to the heavy loss of human life. However, this chapter would be incomplete if the factor which concerns the responsibility of the state authorities was not mentioned. It is, perhaps, the most sensitive, even the most delicate, but also the most important to mention, not so much to use this as a scapegoat than to touch the consciousness of the whole population, in particular the decision-makers. It is not to say that the setbacks would not have been considerable, even by doing all that we could. Even the most advanced countries, and the most capable in the management of natural disasters, have experienced many damages at home. Let us take the recent example of Japan in March 2011 or a less recent example, California in April 1906. Their assessment was not light. Clearly, a country needs to be organized in order to take the necessary measures to protect its population. What can we say?

According to a signed article, in Le Figaro, Chile, is located in one of the most active seismic regions of the world.[6] This republic records on average two earthquakes of 8.5 magnitude every ten years but manages to withstand because of two implemented measures.

a. Earthquake-resistant building standards

b. Preparedness of the population

The austerity in the application of the established principles by the state authorities is what saves the Chileans facing these repeated earthquakes.

For a long time, we must admit that the administrations that have ruled these last decades in Haiti have washed their hands with the thorny question of the urban development and building codes in the country. And the population, taking as approval this leniency, built anywhere, anyhow, with no regard for building standards, and without worry. As a result, we have this massive growth of shanty towns in Port-au-Prince.

I would very much wish that the government could find a working formula to close the floodgate of the unauthorized constructions in Haiti and at the same time, come up with alternate solutions for the most disenfranchised class.

Summary of the buildings destroyed or damaged during the earthquake [7]:

Collapsed or Damaged Houses	Demolished or Damaged Hospitals	Demolished or Damaged Schools
183,383	30	3,978

These data makes you chill!

But from this report, what could we learn for our spiritual life? What lessons can we draw?

A House Built on the Rock

In Matthew 7:24–27, Jesus said:

> Therefore everyone who hears these words of mine and puts them into practice is like a wise man who built his house on the rock.

> The rain came down, the streams rose, and the winds blew and beat against that house; yet it did not fall, because it had its foundation on the rock.

This teaching of Jesus corresponds very well to the subject we talked about—*construction*. The first thing which Jesus puts down is the foundation, the base which has to support the house. One knows that the base is the most important part of any building, even if it is not always the part most considered by laymen. It is rare to hear somebody sharing their first impressions on a house related to the base. It is often the other parts which receive the honor, for example, the architecture, the dimension of rooms, the aesthetics of the bathroom, or the global distribution of the house. Naturally, we are more attracted by the visible part than to the base buried under the ground, but how essential to the resistance of a house—both physically and spiritually. A house devoid of a good foundation is subject to collapse under the slightest shock.

What is it made of this foundation that Jesus is talking about?

Wood? Cement? No!

What is the recipe then? It is to listen to the words of Jesus and to put them into practice. It is simple but very effective. Within the framework of our activities of the ministry, Junie, my wife, and I had the privilege to study the Bible with dozens of people. And the report that we make is that in most of the cases, people are more enthusiastic to do the biblical studies to fill their mind than to want to put into practice the teachings received. And unfortunately, Christians sometimes also lose the good habit of referring to the Scriptures in certain situations and to act accordingly.

In 1992, there was a shortage of gasoline in Haiti. A commercial embargo had been imposed by the international community as an economic sanction in the country, following the military coup that toppled the democratically elected president. As a result, a gallon of gas was being sold for up to 300 gourds ($7 average) in the black market. Needless to mention just how touchy the drivers were about a drop of gasoline. In an attempt to lessen their consumption of gasoline, certain taxi drivers, with passengers on board, used the strategy of coasting. This strategy consisted of turning the engine off while putting the vehicle in neutral and let it roll down the slopes. It was possible because going down, no engine strength was needed to move the car. It was also possible, due to the fact that in Haiti seventy percent of the vehicles have manual transmission. It seems like this trick worked very well for these transport professionals because many of them used the same stratagem.

The Dangerous Side of Coasting

One day, some friends and I went to Fort-Jacques, a historic site located in the hills of Fermathe, one of the suburbs of Pétion-Ville, for an excursion. On the way back after having spending a great time up there, one of my friends, the one who was driving, decided to try the tactic of the taxi drivers to save gas. That's when the car started to spiral at very high speed down the hills. We were panic stricken, when we saw our famous driver fighting unsuccessfully to control and stop the vehicle. Fortunately, there were two big piles of sand on the side of the road, so the driver was able to run the car into one of them. That is what kept us from having an accident that could have been very serious. We were all traumatized by this adventure because we did not expect for this experiment to end so badly. But, we learned our lesson.

What Was the Problem with the Pickup?

We did not know it at the time, but the mechanical system of a vehicle with a diesel engine does not allow this kind of maneuver. When we turned the car off, it locked the braking system and the power steering that helps the driver turn the wheel easily. Thus, with the power turned off, the car became out of control. Frightening!

The point in this story is that as Christians, we cannot under any circumstance have the luxury of turning our spiritual engine off, even for a short time,

> The older we get in our relationship with God, the more we should be careful not to fall into the trap of *"coasting."*

and just coast. Coasting would mean saying or doing what we need to by experience, but without having the right heart. No one is exempt from having these moments of superficiality in their spiritual life. The older we get in our relationship with God, the more we should be careful not to fall into the trap of "coasting." The truth is that after some time in our walk with God, if we are not careful, the activities that we've engaged in all the while can become just rituals that we perform without being aware of their true meaning.

That is the time where the Scriptures begin to be monotonous, even dull, when reading them. That is the time when we start saying some prayers instead of praying. That's also the time when going to church becomes a heavy burden. We arrive last, and we are among the first ones to leave the premises. We forget how to share our faith with others. God is not always the first being who comes to mind when we reap the fruits of our work. There is a Haitian proverb that says, "*Chemen bouton se chemen maleng*" which means, "the road of a pimple is the road to sores." Thus, if your devotion is characterized by these signs, you can be sure that the pimple is big and needs to be treated before it becomes a sore.

Suggested Cure

A—Look for Help

Recognizing that you are in a situation of weakness is a strength that saves. In Matthew 14: 30–31 we read this:

> But when he saw the wind, he was afraid and beginning to sink, cried out, "Lord save me!" Immediately Jesus reached out his hand and caught him. "You of little faith" he said, "Why did you doubt?"

Peter was known as a professional fisherman and a sailor. His job regularly led him to deep waters. Thanks to his experience, he knew the ways to take in the ocean to avoid running aground with his boat. But the apostle had a problem: his performances were conditioned to the whim of the ocean. His human weaknesses were seen as soon as the sea went into frenzy. I should point out that he had, on one hand, accomplished an act that no one else in mankind history had ever accomplished apart from Jesus: that of walking on the water. That is the glorious aspect of the whole scene, where his faith and his courage were emphasized. On the other hand, we saw him drowning himself by focusing on the strength of the wind instead of continuing to fix his eyes on the Master. Fortunately, he had the wit to solicit the help of the Lord. And he was rescued.

This story teaches us two great lessons: a good one and a bad one. The bad is that it is not difficult to be spiritually distracted. And the distractions usually lead to our drowning. And the good one is that it is always possible to get help. We only need to be conscious of that, and raise our hand to make the distress signal.

Therefore, vulnerability becomes an essential element. Can you imagine what would have happened to Peter if he had argued that he was an old fisherman, a regular customer of the unsettled sea? Eventually, he would have found himself under water if he had made a choice to help himself.

Then, let us imitate the example of the apostle Peter. There are brothers and sisters to whom God gave the gift of strengthening the weak. They are wise people who know how to listen, diagnose the problems, and help. Let us seize the opportunity to start all over again, just by making the step to go to those who are appointed for that purpose with an open heart. And God will do the rest.

B—Be Inspired by God's Promises and Wonders

Inspiration is to the Christian what gasoline is to the car. It is inspiration that keeps us on track and motivates us to move forward. In other words, as soon as we cease to be inspired in our relationship with the Lord, we go straight to desiccation and then to abandonment.

One of our main sources of inspiration is definitely the Bible. Through the Holy Scriptures we are provided with all that is necessary to be encouraged. As we read them, we discover all the promises made to us by God. Our faith is also aroused by the demonstration of his love for us at the cross. However, depending on how long we've been walking in faith, the vitamin of inspiration is not always found on the surface of the Scriptures. Hence is the need to learn to dig deeper to improve the quality of our Bible studies. Only at this price can our different needs be met, regardless of our spiritual age.

The Hour Hand

Another source of inspiration comes from our remembrance of the past wonders God has accomplished in our lives. Otherwise, when the blessings and miracles of the past are thrown into the drawer of oblivion, that act becomes an element that can potentially lead us to depletion.

After graduating from primary school in 1977, Jude's mother had offered him a watch as a gift. For a child who was raised in the countryside, receiving a watch at that time was a weighty present. The left arm that wore the jewel was—with pride— held in a strange way as if to say to everyone: *"Have you seen it?"* He had developed the habit of looking at the Timex from time to time, paying particular attention to the needle that marks the second (The second hand).

"But, Jude, why do you look at the watch so often by focusing all that attention on the smallest needle?" an observer asked him one day.

"Because it is a well appreciated reward. My attention to the second hand comes from the fact that it is the only one of the three that, by the evidence of it move- ments, always reassures me that the watch was really working," he replied.

"And what would you have done, Jude, if your watch did not have the second hand?"

"Well! For me it would not be considered a good watch."

"That is an error, my boy! Some watches do not have second hands and are still good," concluded the observer.

We have clearly seen the perception of the young man in rela- tion to the models of watches designed without the second hand. Spiritually, we are sometimes like Jude. We want to feel, hear, or see things move to be certain that something concrete is actually happening in our lives or even that the Lord is with us. Our human side sways naturally toward the sensational, hence the doubt when it is not there. But we must learn that God does not work like the second hand or even as that of the minutes, but rather as that of the hours of our watch. He is at work twenty-four hours a day, even if the receptors of our attention cannot always capture his slow and mysterious progression. So, if we want to be inspired by the work of God in our lives, let us not fix our eyes on the needle itself but on the result of what is accomplished over time. At the end of the day, we will have realized that the turn of the little dial had indeed been carried out. And this will help us to understand that the Lord—although in silence sometimes and at his own pace—always works for our good.

C—Spend Enough Time in Prayer

"And pray in the Spirit on all occasions with all kinds of prayers and requests. With this in mind, be alert and always keep on praying for all the Lord's people" (Ephesians 6:18).

Elsewhere, hadn't Jesus used the parable of the unjust judge to show that we need to pray continuously and not give up (Luke 18:1–8)?

In these two passages, I should point out the expressions: *at all time*, *always pray*, *complete perseverance*, and *not give up* showing the mindset of consistency that is required for this spiritual discipline.

It is not praying every now and then that will move mountains; it is neither the prayers offered routinely that would move God.

Thus, to live a prayerful life is the standard to which we are called to push ourselves if we want to be close to the Lord, know his will, and be able to see miracles fulfilled in our lives.

D—Seek First the Kingdom and Righteousness of God

This is the idea of developing a total worship toward God. The Latin word that corresponds to worship is *devotio-onis* which means dedication. We live in a world where unfortunately the order of priorities is inverted by the majority. Our jobs, our studies, and the long list of our activities are placed first. Then, we add a little of God's service when we feel that the circumstances permit it.

Nevertheless, according to God's plan, the first place should be granted to the Kingdom and righteousness of God (Matthew 6:33). A certain determination is needed to make this scripture our pet project.

When I got to Boston with my family in 2014, everything was to be learned a new country, a different temperature, a new culture, another language, and an unusual operating rate. We were challenged in the aspect of our worship to God.

> If we want to be inspired by the work of God in our lives, let us not fix our eyes on the needle itself but on the result of what is accomplished over time. At the end of the day, we would realize that the turn of the little dial had indeed been carried out. And this will help us to understand that the Lord— although in silence sometimes and at his own space—always acts for our good.

The first winter we lived in New England was a real test of conviction. By joining the Boston church, I had to practice as a disciple certain values that I had taught as an evangelist in Haiti. For example, I always told the assembly not to allow rain to keep them from coming to worship Services. I am talking about a congregation of several hundred members where only approximately 8 percent had the privilege of a car. I encouraged them to have an umbrella or a plastic cover. But I did not know the cost of applying such a teaching because I was a member of that small group of fortunate people. The experience of that first winter in Boston gave us the opportunity to fully understand what going to church when the weather was not favorable meant.

To be honest, I must admit that we couldn't wait to see the snow fall when we arrived. Our curiosity was especially fed by our friends who, quite often, asked us the question "Have you already seen the snow fall?" It had become one of my children's favorite subjects. They often talked about snowmen. And, as adults, we were ready to take some beautiful pictures. When the lady came, however, it turned a storm well dressed in its white dress that put everybody on high alert instead.

According to an article entitled: "Survival guide in Boston, after several snowstorms," Mathilde, the editor, discloses, and I quote:

> Imagine a buildup of 1.80 meters of snow, in less than twenty days. That's what fell in Boston, and it does not seem to want to stop for the moment. It is a historic record for the city, although used to the snow in winter. The buildup was such that year that the situation did not longer seem to be under control at the beginning of the week . . . The Governor declared several snow days that paralyzed the city those last days. The children do not have school for a week. Small shops and restaurants sometimes have to close. Garbage is not collected in the central districts, we are asked to work from home, people have to sleep at their workplace, and the traffic is unbearable for the motorists (Even forbidden in case of emergency). [8]

For a family that came from a tropical country, the adaptation to the climate change was not easy. It is true that we had waited for the snow, but it was not to be buried under it. The Bostonians told us, "Ah! Your break-in was terrible." And they were right.

The Challenging Aspect of Our Worship

Some Sundays, it was necessary to wake up early to face the brutality of the cold when the temperature had dropped, so I could clean the parking lot to clear the exit way and then prepare the family to go to church. The scenario was the same for certain midweek services. It was challenging, I'll admit. It takes a lot of determination not to become a lukewarm Christian in this environment where all the conditions are gathered in such a state of mind. Imagine, you are inside a house that is comfortably heated, you have electricity twenty-four hours a day, you have access to dozens of television channels, you have the Internet that connects you to the world through social media, and in addition you do not have a police officer behind you who would force you to leave your comfort at the time of the services. Then, what would push you to join the assembly of the church when it is cold outside? Only our love for the Kingdom of God.

The Temptation

I clearly remember a Sunday morning when it snowed in big flakes. I kept watching my phone, wondering if the leaders had not, as they had done it another time, sent a message to cancel the service of that morning. But, the leadership staff did not think it necessary. And at that point, the temptation to leave our seats empty had reached its highest level. I told myself, when the church notices our absence, they will remember that we just arrived in the country and that we had not adjusted ourselves to the low temperature and the practice of cleaning off the parking lot to go to the church yet. What a beautiful excuse I came up with!

As soon as we hesitate to make the effort that Jesus would make in our place for the service of God, all types of excuses will come most naturally to calm the voice of our conscience until our walk with the Lord is reduced to a second-hand devotion under the effect of repetition. At that point, it is necessary to fight to avoid adopting such a standard as a normal one.

The Language Barrier

Another challenge for us was the language barrier in attending the worship service, where everything was said in a language that was not ours. When the evangelist told a joke that made everybody laugh, my wife and I looked at each other with an inquiring eye without being able to enjoy it. In the fellowship, our conversations with those who did not speak our language were limited. It took months of listening and perseverance before we were able to understand 70 percent of the messages and felt at ease.

> As soon as we hesitate to make the effort that Jesus would make in our place for the service of God, all types of excuses will come most naturally to calm the voice of our conscience until our walk with the Lord is reduced to a second-hand devotion under the effect of repetition.

Our new situation was difficult, but that could not be taken as an excuse not to look for God's presence with my family. What we especially needed by going to worship God was neither to speak nor to understand the human languages—although important for the enlightenment—but, it is mainly to speak the worship language *in spirit and truth*. Such is the unique criterion required for a true worshipper (John 4: 23–24). At least we were able to dance in singing. When the songs were not projected onto the screen, we sang them in our own language with some moderation to not disturb the atmosphere. The most important is that we had given our hearts in spite of our barriers.

Nobody has the makings of a Christian without fault, but I am always afraid at the thought of being seen by God as a son who serves him without being really committed. Because of that, I always want to do my best to dismiss the frivolous and deliberate decisions that could—now or in the future—negatively influence the rhythm of my personal walk with God. All that it takes is the decision to put God first.

What was the epilogue of that Sunday of snow about which I spoke earlier? It fortunately came to me the idea of calling a brother, and that family picked us up to go together to worship.

My conviction is that there is a thing that remains unchanged and unchangeable: even when our lives take other turns, it is the expectation of the Lord for us to move toward his Word. Here or over there, yesterday or today, we are always called to have a first-class devotion for the Lord. Then, let us together make the effort to set the clocks to the right time in our Christian lives. It is an adventure that can sometimes appear difficult but is building on the rock and saying no to coasting.

An Incomplete House Becomes a Relic

There is another message that Jesus gives us on the subject of building:

> Suppose one of you wants to build a tower. Won't you first sit down and estimate the cost to see if you have enough money to complete it? For if you lay the foundation and are not able to finish it, everyone who sees it will ridicule you, saying, "this person began to build and wasn't able to finish." (Luke 14: 28–30)

Here, Jesus calls us to count the cost to see if we can finish the construction that we have started. Some take this call as a loophole to say, "I don't feel ready because . . ." The excuses can be many. However, what is required through this passage it is not the feeling of being ready to begin to build, but rather the determination to finish once we put our hand to the plow. I have seen people who thought that they were ready because they felt it, but, during the twenty-five years that God has given me in his family, I have watched the fall of a lot of soldiers along the way. My prayer is that they can regain their position.

No one can ignore his feelings since we are created like this, but in the big decisions that affect our lives in the long run, we have to watch out because our feelings are not always consistent. What makes us lose our mind today can tomorrow leave us very indifferent and vice versa; however, the reason that compels us to follow Jesus should itself be convincing and final. Therefore, when our feelings change, taking away the heartfelt desire to remain at the foot of the Lord, the reason of the cross should bring us back on track and make us do the opposite. Since this is the most legitimate and important act that a person can perform to meet one of his essential needs, spiritually speaking, we should never go back on it. Jesus' challenge is to not make this decision lightly.

Counting the Cost in Real Life

Even in everyday life, let's say we are qualified to buy ourselves a house, one cannot go at it blindly. This is an important investment that requires us to look at all the angles and to review and understand before signing the terms with the financial institution. This is counting the cost.

Why? Because this is going to have a certain impact on our lives. It takes time, sometimes decades, to pay off the mortgage with all sorts of consequences and often financially painful ones. Therefore, if we don't count the cost really well, we risk being frustrated over time. The worst case is that when we end up losing the house because we cannot fulfill the obligations for which we had committed ourselves. Not only do we lose the house, we also forfeit the money we had already paid all those years. This is a real blow to families and marriages.

It is the same thing that happens to us when we commit ourselves to follow Jesus without considering the real implications of such a commitment. Some gave up because they were discouraged. Others because they had been wounded by members of the body. Who would be able to live here on earth without—at times—being discouraged? Or without getting hurt or hurting? We can do all we can to protect ourselves, but hurt will find a way to reach us and go from us to others. On occasion, without realizing it, a little gesture, a look, a joke, or even silence can hurt. In this way, it does not take much to offend or be offended. It is true that we are all sensitive to certain things and eventually with good reason. However, when the tongue is bitten by the teeth or burned by hot food, it does not remove itself from the mouth. Sometimes, it is even injured repeatedly and in the same spot. One finds the tongue sad to the point of not being able to fully play its role in the chewing and swallowing of food. In spite of everything, it remains attached to the place where God has planted it until it is cured of its irritation. Otherwise, many of us would be deprived of this small, but important, organ of our make-up. Inasmuch as these incidents occur every day at the level of our buccal cavity, I dare say that the tongue is a good example of a faithful component of the mouth. Teeth are extracted or replaced by the dentist due to ailments. However, the tongue, despite its vulnerability and frequent discomforts, always reaches the end point of the race, knowing that it was chosen not to be anywhere else but inside the mouth.

The Example of the Tongue

Discouraged, we hang in there. Wounded, we resolve the problem, but we do not give up. It may take time and energy to keep staying faithful, but we don't quit. We must remember that the most important for the adversary is not the color of the weapon that makes us fall, but its power to reach us. Since, for him, all means are good so long as they are able to derail us or to stop us in the race with the final purpose to prevent us from seeing our God. It is up to us to decide today that he will not find in his entire arsenal any weapon, which will bring us down from the tree where we are perched in faith, no matter what happens.

Build the house! It is Jesus' dearest wish for us; however, he doesn't want us to build solely based on our emotions or superficial interests. That is why he invites us to count the cost, to abide by the standards that he has set for us to guarantee the stability that we all seek.

The Insurance

Who would own a house without insurance? Nowadays, the insurance companies play a major role in all spheres of modern life. We all want to have a certain guarantee on all our purchases, whether they are small like an iPad, mid-range like a car, or significant like a house. We are ready to pay a fee to have the assurance that if our belongings were to get damaged, they could be repaired or replaced.

One of the first requirements that the financial institutions present to the customers in the process of financing their project is an insurance policy for the relevant items; otherwise a loan would not be approved.

I learned recently in an informal way that a number of sports superstars pay a lot in order to insure certain parts of their body. For example, according to this source, Leo Messi, one of the best soccer players over the world would have a special coverage for his left foot, because 80 percent of all his sporting achievements depend on that leg. I was fascinated by the idea that the insurance companies could offer such option. Now then, you see, we are willing to pay, and sometimes a lot, to make sure that everything is covered: our life, our health, our livestock, our real estate, and so forth. This simply means that we all understand the value of insurance. From then on, a win-win system is drawn up: We give them our money, and they, in return, give us peace of mind.

Therefore, if we place this much trust in human insurance, how much more should we believe in the assurance that Jesus offers us? He told us clearly that if our house is built on the Rock, it will not be destroyed. What else do we need to hear?

Hit by the streams and the rains? Yes! Buffeted by the winds and the earthquakes? Yes! But destroyed by them? *No!*

The insurance that we are offered through Jesus is a package which far exceeds any other one on earth. It is not designed to replace what would possibly be destroyed, but it rather aims to prevent any spiritual destruction knocking at our doors. Thus, the only charge that we have toward Jesus is to give him our hearts, so that he can work, ensuring us a blissful eternity in return.

The 1993 Nobel Peace prize winner, Nelson Mandela said *that he never loses—either he wins, or he learns*. This famous sentence becomes even truer for those who decide to listen to Jesus' words and put them into practice. There is no possible defeat, and that guarantees we have it even beyond the terrestrial boundaries. Isn't that incredible?

My Father-in-Law's House

After having spent seven good months in the tents in the relief camp of the church at Canapé-Vert, I had to leave the camp following the advice of a big spiritual brother. My family and I were welcomed by my father-in-law in Delmas. His house had come out unscathed by God's grace. Yet, something had captured my interest from the very first moment: the exceptional condition of my father-in-law's house in the aftermath of the events.

Listed among the Safe Houses

The ministry of public works (MPW) had set up a program of evaluation of the houses that were still standing to determine their level of safety. They were placed in three categories. Those that were completely damaged were marked in red, which meant that these houses were to be rebuilt. Those who were fair were marked in yellow, which meant that they are salvageable with repairs. And the others had the green mark, which meant that they could be lived in now, without worry. And what was more intriguing in my father-in-law's house was not the fact that it was listed on the third group, but rather because I had not noticed any trace of cracks on the walls, both interior and exterior. I was able to notice it at first sight because I had seen other houses that were also part of the list of viable houses which still, however, carried the mark of the cataclysm albeit a light crackle in the floor, the ceiling or on the walls. Needless to say, I was a bit curious as to the origin of this difference.

**MY FATHER-IN-LAW'S HOUSE WITHOUT ANY REPAIR
AFTER THE EARTHQUAKE (PHOTO TAKEN IN 2016)**

The Secret Unveiled

One afternoon, my father-in-law and I were together on the third-floor balcony. It was a house built in three split levels. We were observing the entire area and commenting on the tragedy still fresh and vivid in every citizen's mind. I was offered the opportunity to ask my father-in-law the burning question: Why is it that in the same community some houses were totally destroyed, others very damaged, and yours remained standing without the slightest crack?

I still remember the pride with which he explained things to me. He answered me:

> My dear Jo, when the engineer started the work, to tell you the truth, I had serious doubts about him because I did not understand what he was doing. For three consecutive weeks, while visiting the construction site after work, I had realized that the work had not progressed far enough to justify the expenses. It is true; I

saw a lot of activity, but no obvious signs of progress. I was frustrated to the point I had begun to think that the materials were being resold in my absence. The workers, it seemed to me, were wasting their time, pretending to work to lengthen the workdays, being that they were paid on a daily basis. I had all kinds of negative thoughts about the engineer and his construction crew. Puzzled, I questioned the engineer who cleared things up for me and calmed my heart.

Here is the explanation that the engineer gave me.

The ground was not suited for such a large-scale construction, and the first layer of soil to a depth of five or six feet was vaporous, so we had to dig deeper to reach a solid layer where the real work of the foundation began. Although it is taking time and a lot of material to treat this type of soil and to install the strip footings underground before we can finish the foundation, don't worry, Mr. Timot, you will have a solid house. It is better to take the time along the way and then to receive good news.

My father-in-law shared with me that he was encouraged by the explanation of the engineer, but he remained convinced that he was abused in thinking that the materials he provided to have the job done had been stolen. However, when the tragedy occurred, he then understood the deeper meaning of the explanation of the engineer, twenty-five years later.

"I lost my store in the earthquake." He added, "and if I were to also lose the house, what would I do at my age of eighty-seven years?" He just sighed.

Oftentimes, our attitude toward God is not different than that of my father-in-law towards his engineer. Sometimes, because we do not understand the way God wants to work in our houses, we don't respond well in our attitude or in our action. For example, isn't it too difficult to remain pure sexually before marriage while in a dating relationship? To always tell the truth—isn't that too difficult? Today, as in the past, many are saying, *"This is a hard teaching. Who can accept it?"* (John 6:60).

While in reality, it is obvious that what is really hard today is not Jesus' messages, but what happens in our lives when this message is rejected. I am referring here to the situations, which annihilate us inside and leave us hopeless. We may not understand the rules that God calls us to follow, but our lack of understanding does not diminish the seriousness and the depth of what He wants to accomplish in our marriages, our families, and our communities. And, our part of the task is not to try to understand all the details, but to develop the necessary confidence in what he is doing and to be obedient. Sooner or later, the results will be clear to us, as it was for my father-in-law after the disaster.

"Today, I would have liked to see this engineer again to thank him, but also to confess the bad thoughts that I had about him and to apologize to him. But, I do not know what became of him because I have not seen him in years, and I don't even remember his name," my father-in-law confessed to me.

Here Is the Big Picture of the Story

At the time of the earthquake on January 12, 2010, my father-in-law was not at home. He was on his way back from his shop when the earth began to tremble. Having been exactly in the neighborhood of the courthouse downtown, he witnessed the gigantic building collapse. In the same area, the National Palace and the main office of the General Direction of Taxes had collapsed. He also saw the fall of a number of houses, which apparently were very solid, on the way to his home that same evening. He had the big concern all the way that his house must have had the same fate as the others. And this thought lingered the entire journey until he arrived to his destination. But once he got home, he was delighted to see that the house was still standing. He could not go inside yet to have a closer look because no one would have taken that risk with the continued aftershocks. As soon as things calmed down a little, he went in and what he saw left him speechless.

A week later, say January 20, there was in the early hours another earthquake that shook Port-au-Prince. It was of 6.1 magnitude on the Richter scale, [9] but it was talked about very little in the press because we were still recovering from the first one. But it was still strong enough to give the final blow to more buildings that were partially destroyed by the first one. And for that one, my father-in-law was inside the house when everybody was rushing outside to seek cover. He stayed in his room because his health and his age kept him from being able to run like the others. When evening came, his children tried to convince him to leave the house as a precautionary measure. He simply answered that he was going to stay and even if he had to die, he would die there. "For my age," he argued, "I am tired of going up and down the stairs." Also because of his asthma, he didn't want to expose himself to the cold night. Thus, to stay inside was his final decision. And that is where he lived during the majority of the aftershocks that followed the actual earthquake.

Besides the two main earthquakes, do you know how many tremors were recorded for the period of January 12 to 24 of 2010? They were a total number of fifty-two marked greater than or equal to 4.5 on the Richter scale. And the good news is that for all these tremors, big or small, my father-in-law's house was able to withstand them all. Wow! What victory!

Why?

Because first of all, God wanted things to be this way, but secondly because twenty-five years ago, the engineer in charge of the work had done what needed to be done at the foundation level, so that the house could stand the test successfully.

Do you remember how frustrated he was at the beginning? Now, he was able to enjoy the product of what had caused his frustration when he had to pay the price that was necessary at that time to end up with this remarkable performance. What a great lesson!

It is important to see that this is the same thing that Jesus does for us through his Word and his sacrifice on the cross. There will be the main bursts followed by the aftershocks that will fall upon our house (personal life, marriage, family, etc.), but if we agree to pay the price by overcoming the frustration and the fear that haunts us for wanting to place our lives in God's hand, the house will not collapse in the name of Jesus because his method is tested and proven solid.

The Bad Choice

Not to obey the Word of God is also a choice that unfortunately many people make. Some of them admit openly that they want nothing to do with the Bible or the church. They are skeptical about the Gospel and proclaim to be atheists.

For others, their reluctance comes sometimes as a result of a bad past experience.

There is still another category of people who go to a kind of church, and attend many religious activities, but who do not know the real way. This is a big deal spiritually. Paul said in this regard:

For I can testify about them that they are zealous for God, but their zeal is not based on knowledge. Since they did not know the righteousness of God and sought to establish their own, they did not submit to God's righteousness. (Romans 10:2–3).

The Consequences Related to Our Bad Choices

Why should we refrain from choosing not to take the Word of God seriously? Jesus said:

But everyone who hears these words of mine and does not put them into practice is like a foolish man who built his house on sand. 27 The rain came down, the streams rose, and the winds blew and beat against that house, and it fell with a great crash. (Matthew 7:26–27)

Natural disasters strike all houses with the same strength without any exception. Only a solid foundation enables us to resist the blows.

The Amount of Rubble and Debris Picked Up

Do you want to know the amount of rubbles and debris that was picked up after the earthquake from the wreckage of the houses destroyed in Haiti?

Not less than thirty millions cubic meters of rubble and garbage of all types throughout the city of only Port-au-Prince, not to mention Léogane and Jacmel. That is an enormous amount, isn't it?

Do you want to know the amount of rubble that still remains of the wreckage of houses destroyed from a spiritual point of view?

Look around you and see the number of people who are under the influence of drug, alcohol, and sexual depravation. Marriage, this sacred covenant, is distorted today and trivialized to its lowest level. The number of divorces is increasing more and more according to the statistics. Depression is going through the roof in the families and does not spare our youth. According to a report released by the World Health Organization in 2014, one person commits suicide every forty seconds. That makes roughly 800,000 persons who take their own lives annually [11]. These are alarming data. This is an undeniable sign of a world discouraged by all sorts of ups and downs.

All these clues are the result of spiritual foundations undermined by our refusal to practice the Word of God in our lives, without any distinction whether we go to church or not.

Who would like to see his house in this pile of rubble and waste? No one! No one!

So, let's all choose to build our houses better, both those that inhabit us and those that shelter us.

An example of rubble left by the earthquake of 2010 in Haiti

CHAPTER 3

THE DISCOVERED TREASURE

THE DISCOVERED TREASURE

> No temptation has overtaken you except what is common to mankind. And God is faithful; he will not let you be tempted beyond what you can bear. But when you are tempted, he will also provide a way out so that you can endure it. (1 Corinthians 10:13)

There is no better passage to introduce this chapter than this one. This scripture reminds us of the faithfulness of God in difficult times with a promise to provide a way out so that we can endure it.

As a reminder, I would say that it was a very big shock for the whole Haitian community—both those in the Diaspora and locally—when the country was hit by the earthquake. The last two generations did not know much about earthquakes. We have obviously heard about them and definitely read about them, but this kind of natural disaster does not appear in the list of those, which usually make the headlines in Haiti like hurricanes, floods, and landslides.

The last earthquake that really wreaked havoc in Haiti before that of January 12, 2010 goes back to the eighteenth century. You understand now the total disconnection in our human life with this phenomenon, but also the weakness in our capacity to manage it.

I admit that the equation was very complex to solve from a human point of view. All at once, life had stopped in Haiti. The earthquake kept freeing his energy, through strong and frequent retorts. The sounds that it produced (goodoo-goodoo) added to thousands of other shouts of people who were screaming everywhere for help, were deafening. The whole population was in the streets. People helped one another as wounded persons were taken as a matter of urgency toward hospital centers. The people who were not in their houses hurried to get back to their homes to see what had happened to their families. The traffic was impossible. To go on foot had become as a passage obliged for everybody. Besides the carnival, only the earthquake was so well able to fuse all the sectors of the society like that. The only difference was that this time, it was not for dancing but to face their confusion together.

Meanwhile, what could lead to tracks of relief was fundamentally a member of unknown elements of the equation. I am referring to roads, the electric grid, and communication, which were all cut at that moment. It was total confusion. There was blood almost everywhere. A thick smoke of dust showed in the sky of Port-au-Prince. We could have the strange sensation that we had left the real human world, to find ourselves abruptly in another imaginary one, where everything was going fast and in the wrong direction. Indescribable! But, it is often when we find ourselves at the lowest point in life, without strength and without weapons or solutions, that the loyalty of God can be more obviously felt.

David said in Psalm 29, "The Lord shakes the Desert of Kadesh," but in verse 11 he added, "He gives strength to his people; the Lord blesses his people with peace." In this situation, the church in Haiti and in particular that of

Port-au-Prince saw the Scriptures come alive. No grief without relief as the saying goes. In all the details, we felt the hand of God working in our favor.

In What Aspect of the Crisis Did We See God's Grace the Most?

Emotionally

Unexplainably, a great number of Christians, particularly those who used to live not far from the church property and some others who were stuck in the surroundings, automatically came to the premises of the church. It was like we had an appointment in the hours following the earthquake. And that is how our relief shelter started on the church's premise in Canapé-Vert.

There were about ten of us to arrive first, so we began to sing and pray to ask the Lord to help us. It was a prayer he fully answered when you consider all that we went through from then to the end of the tunnel.

The first nights were spent in the open in the camp in Canapé-Vert.

In Psalm 23, David said in the first 4 verses, *The Lord is my shepherd, I lack nothing. He makes me lie down in green pastures, he leads me beside quiet waters, he refreshes my soul.*

Elsewhere, the prophet Isaiah said in chapter 40 in verses 10 and 11:

> See, the Sovereign Lord comes with power, and he rules with a mighty arm. See, his reward is with him, and his recompense accompanies him. He tends his flock like a shepherd: He gathers the lambs in his arms and carries them close to his heart; he gently leads those that have young.

This God who David had described as a shepherd and who Isaiah had also described the same had also been a good shepherd for us in these difficult circumstances as well. The small group of ten had grown and had reached roughly 150 to become the main relief shelter of the church, next to the one in Carrefour and the one behind the airport.

From this moment on, another page of our history as a church was on the verge of being written. It was the page (of Acts 2:44, 46) that was replicated:

> All the believers were together and had everything in common. Every day they continued to meet together in the temple courts. They broke bread in their homes and ate together with glad and sincere hearts.

Yes, we were all together in the same place, eating together, working together, and offering devotion to the Lord together. And this time, it wasn't for the two or three measly hours of the Sunday or the midweek service, but a period of well over several months. It was incredible to see the faithfulness of God reflected in such detail. At least we were able to mobilize and to be together at this crucial moment. It would have been more difficult for us and even stressful if we each had to fend for ourselves alone. But by coming together as brothers and sisters in Christ, we felt supported and strengthened emotionally. Isn't that grace! God was working in this condition of despair to restore hope in the hearts of those who belong to him.

To put it into perspective, I would say that we all carried the aftereffects of the earthquake in our hearts by losing at least one person who was dear to us. Some lost several. The emotional impact was rigorous for everyone, even when we realized that it was worse for some. But in addition to that, a few carried the aftereffects in their body by being injured because they were affected physically. So by dwelling together, those who needed medical care could be assisted, and those who had lost a member of their family could find listening ears, comfort, and encouragement.

Isn't God *faithful*?

Doc La

I would like to digress on the aspect of the care of the wounded to show you the faithfulness of God. Just imagine the scene of a demolished city. The handful of hospitals that were able to accommodate the wounded were full and could not take any more. The brothers and sisters who were doctors in the church and who fervently and routinely served the community and the brothers and sisters through the clinic of Hope Worldwide were hindered because they too were affected and needed help as well. This explained their absence in the relief shelter camp the first days.

However, Junie, my wife, had hardly finished training in first-aid care, and she was the one who put on her gloves to make use of all that she had learned in this seminar. The training was still fresh in her memory because the disaster took place four days before her graduation. Twice a day, "Doc la," as she was nick-named by her patients, made her round in the camp to dress all the cuts and wounds, big and small. Healthcare had become a scarce commodity in a capital filled with sick people, deprived of a third of its healthcare professionals. I thank God that she was in a position to bring this small contribution in the first days before others could join her to form a medical team. She not only served the campers, she was requested by others of the neighborhood because the demand was very high for health care, and she carried out her task with great enjoyment.

Why do I mention this? To show the faithfulness of God more than the service provided by the servant. Initially, in one of our conversations, Junie expressed her desire to take some classes in first-aid care. She wanted to be trained to help the family, but especially our two boys. The eldest, Jova, has sensitive allergenic skin that had often caused some mild wounds on his legs; the younger, Elie, had repeated nosebleeds. When the earthquake occurred, we all clearly understood that it was God who had put that thought on our sister's heart, not just for the biological family, but also for the other one that God had given us, our spiritual family.

Where did she manage to find the much-needed materials to help people? Fortunately, the room of the clinic of HOPE was not destroyed by the earthquake. Here, also, we saw God's faithfulness. Because it was a functional clinic, all the necessary equipment was available to provide first aid to those who needed it.

To God be the glory!

Physically

The next day being January 13, 2010, we started a new day together. After the morning devotional, we attempted to outline how we would address this crisis. This was something we had never experienced before. At that time, the idea of preparing something for everybody to eat or just for the children was put on the discussion table. It was the first thing we envisioned as a pressing need.

Hence the Questions: What and How?

In the Gospel of Mark chapter 6, there's the story of the five thousand that were fed by Jesus. Let's look at what verses 30–37 say:

> The apostles gathered around Jesus and reported to him all they had done and taught. Then, because so many people were coming and going that they did not even have a chance to eat, he said to them, "Come with me by yourselves to a quiet place and get some rest."

> So they went away by themselves in a boat to a solitary place. But many who saw them leaving recognized them and ran on foot from all the towns and got there ahead of them. When Jesus landed and saw a large crowd, he had compassion on them, because they were like sheep without a shepherd. So he began teaching them many things.

> By this time it was late in the day, so his disciples came to him. "This is a remote place," they said, "and it's already very late. Send the people away so that they can go to the surrounding countryside and villages to buy themselves something to eat."

But he answered, "You give them something to eat."

They said to him, "That would take more than half a year's wage! Are we to go and spend that much on bread and give it to them to eat?"

We referred to this scripture because to some degree there was similarity of needs and environment in this regard. The need for food was felt both for the disciples and for the crowd that was gathered around Jesus to hear his teaching. However, we have to admit that circumstances were not favorable to meet the need of that moment. Two obstacles were to be considered for the realization of such a project, the fact of being in a desert and the size of the crowd. These two situations made it difficult to find a suitable solution. The disciples suggested to send the people away, so they could find something to eat, and Jesus answered for them to meet this need themselves.

What! The disciples couldn't be more stunned. And the questions that they raised were proof of their shock: *"Are we to go and spend that much on bread and give it to them to eat?"*

These questions show clearly that they didn't have faith. Nevertheless, we also ask these kinds of questions when we doubt that something is possible. Isn't this true?

Let's wait and see what the Bible tells us at this point.

But, to the question of the disciples in verse 37, let's expand the scope to consider an element that could be taken as an explanation of their unbelief. Remember, besides the fact that they were hungry and tired themselves, they were now called by the master to solve this feeding of the crowd in a remote place in the desert.

The Logistics in the Desert

Let's assume that after having verified with Judas the treasurer of the group, the two hundred denarii had been available for the purchase of bread, how would they manage to get such a big quantity of bread to this deserted place? It was not the era of the Internet that would have offered them the option of placing an online order with a free home delivery. It was not the era of pickup to delegate two or three disciples of the group to go to the city in the small van with the special mission to purchase what was needed to feed the crowd. From a logistical point of view, the challenge was significant, and the twelve had understood it well.

According to the free encyclopedia, from the time of the Roman Empire, especially under Augustus, the adopted son of Julius Caesar, a pound of bread was sold to one As (Roman currency). Two hundred denarii would provide two thousand (2000) pounds of bread, since denarii was equivalent to ten As. If we were still using the denarii, it does not undergo any economic variation with time, in assuming also that a pound never changes, that kind of money would yield us approximately one thousand three hundred thirty three (1333) loaves of bread (large size) with twenty-four slices per bag. In a way, the disciples could see this as a staggering logistical problem in all regards, and that is why dismissing the crowd seemed like the simplest decision to make.

You and I often react the same way. We have the natural tendency to avoid all that may seem difficult to manage. We do not always want to venture, if we are not sure beforehand, when we are not in control of all the components of the assembly. But, experiences have shown that we do not receive our best sessions of training from God when we master everything on the easy road. On the contrary, uncertainties and deficiencies are often the tools used on the field to form our character. But as our coach, God knows when we need to breathe, to exercise our muscles, and also when to end a session of training. All we have to do is to fix our eyes on Him, by trusting Him when we are right in the middle of our own deserts.

The Exercise of Faith When Everything Seems Dark

Feeding a crowd in a deserted place appeared impossible for the disciples, but it did not prevent Jesus from asking them to go through this test of faith. Today, aren't we called to come out of our comfort zone and to venture?

For example, this book that you hold in your hand now could have come out back in 2012, and guess what held me back? Unbelief. Doubt challenged me: *"You want to write a book? Don't be ridiculous, Jean-Jorel. Do what you know how to do my friend, and don't try to go beyond that. I wonder if, I wonder if . . ."*

Let me confess that the little voice that whispered to me convinced me that I was incapable of such an endeavor and made me lose five years. Twice I attempted again, and the same voice was heard to make me stop. Finally, encouraged by Junie, I decided after much reluctance to resume writing the book and to finish it, without knowing first what that would take.

Maybe you are hearing this same voice today. Do not listen to it. Otherwise, you will not ever explore your real potential and discover your hidden talents. The Word of God defines faith for us in saying that *Now faith is confidence in what we hope for an assurance about what we do not see* (Hebrews 11:1).

How this dream did become a reality actually?

I Had in My Mind the Exact Picture of the Book That I Wanted to Write

It is easy to feel like those people, who when they go to the store to buy themselves a product, cannot make a choice because of the large number of possibilities at their disposal. They can remain in the dark for a long time about what they really want. But, if we want to go somewhere, we have to get a clear sense of the targeted objective. There is nothing wrong with us taking our time to study all the possibilities and to come to terms with the best option. But, at the end of the day, we can have an outline like this one:

- O = the targeted objective

- E = the elements we have initially

- P = the plan that will connect E to O

- F = the faith, as the key of success.

Keep in mind the targeted objective, and combining the elements we have with faith, go forward with the plan God gives us to meet the objective.

Otherwise, how will it become a reality? We often spend more time worrying about material and financial things that are needed for the implementation of our projects instead of spending time working on the plan with God's help.

It is important to understand that even if little or no material to meet the need, the power of God can still accomplish the impossible once you have the necessary faith. For example, in the story of five thousand men fed by Jesus, how many loaves of bread and fishes did He make available at his disposal in the desert? In this case, the five loaves of bread and two fishes—considered the elements at hand—were insignificant in regard to the number of people to be fed. But by God's power, the miracle was achieved.

Once we have the plan and it is approved by God, He will bring all the essential resources. All we need is an objective, a plan, and God's approval to start. So don't approach your projects by putting the cart before the horse.

I Submitted It to God in Prayer

The second phase is to submit our plans to God through prayer. Once we are clear on the project that we want to realize, we have to present it to God while waiting for clear signs that come from His will. *Ask and it will be given to you; seek and you will find; knock and the door will be opened to you* (Matthew 7:7).

The prayers made with explanatory details of the what, when, how, and why can be more effective than general prayers that do not send the request in an objective and specific way. So I prayed:

> Lord, You know that I am not a professional writer, but I would like to be able to show things that you accomplished in my personal life and in that of my family and in the church in Haiti before, during, and after the earthquake. If I preach about them, it would only reach a restricted number of people, but if I write them, more people will know that you really did extraordinary things in Haiti. Be with my hand to write and be also with my heart to release what must be imprinted, please. In the name of Jesus I ask you this, Amen!

This was my typical prayer with certain adjustments every time I had to work on this book.

Seek Counsel and Act

This is the stage which demonstrates our faith. Do actions that lead us closer to our objective every day, without omitting to look for advice (Proverbs 15: 22). For example, for this book, the first initiative I took was to buy notebooks and pencils. When I got back to the house, I began by transferring the notes that I had already written in an old notebook, which would form the basis of my first chapter. From then on, I set out to work relentlessly.

Whoever wants to see his dream realized should never be short of actions, even to the point of exhaustion.

> Whoever wants to see his dream realized should never be short of actions, even to the point of exhaustion.

As I decided to look for advice and act, I called a good friend one day to tell him that I was writing a book on the things that I learned in Haiti through the earthquake. This friend encouraged me on this initiative that I was to make a feather on a hen and advised me to type up directly on the computer to save time. What he told me was definitely wholesome advice, but I was challenged by my limitation on computer skills. I could verify my e-mail and send short messages, but to type a long manuscript, I had to recognize that I had no mastery of the keyboard nor the speed suited to execute such task. So how did I respond to this challenging advice?

I had my laptop repaired of a small problem, and I put aside the notebooks and pen and did all the work directly on the computer. It took me time to get there, much time, but going out of our comfort zone has a price—that of having the patience to navigate on an unknown field, to learn something different— but, the work was completed by the divine hand. I definitely became more skillful.

Nicolas Boileau's words echo this process: "Twenty times on the job, put your work down, polish it ceaselessly, and re-polish it, sometimes add to it and often erase."

Thus, retain these words: *objective, plan, prayers, advice, and action.*

Dream and Faith—Warning

We have every right to dream and to develop some faith for our dreams. I believe that it is important to have a plan for these dreams and to follow this plan. However, I believe that it is even more important to understand that we can do every- thing by following the best recipe and still not reach the tar- geted objective. Then, if the doors close on your projects after having done all this is within your power it may be an answer from God, meaning this is for later or simply the answer *no*. Be careful that the disappointment does not affect your faith to the point of causing you to not dream. It is not when the most desired and costly thing comes true that reveals our real level of faith, but rather it is when the request, which packs in all our dreams, is refused that God says "*my grace is enough for you*" (2 Corinthians 12:9). There lies the real test of our confidence in Him. I have seen people full of potential withdraw their faith after being empty-handed during their first or even their second try. Declaring themselves defeated, they agree to evolve far below their real potential than to keep daring. Everything is filtered by their ability to detect at a distance all that they cannot control the situation, and then, they become paralyzed by the fear of the failure that haunts their spirit. They are at a disadvantage because they lack the optimism to succeed by the means of our faithful God, if such is His will.

"If you want to see what you have never seen; you must start by doing what you have never done" (a quote of the late Mohammed Ali).

Do you know what John's Gospel says about the same story of five loaves? It was Jesus who asked Philip, "Where shall we buy bread so that these people will have it to eat?" (John 6:5–10) The Bible mentions that Jesus was saying this *"to test him because he knew what He was going to do."*

The truth is that we all have our difficulties, and we always will. When one is resolved, another appears, and then another. The stairway we climb sometimes seems to lack the very next steps needed for the conquest of our aspirations. Do not lose confidence. For God

> It is not when the most desired and costly thing comes true that reveals our real level of faith, but rather it is when the request, which packs in all our dreams, is refused that God says "My grace is enough for you" (2 Corinthians 12:9). There, lies the real test of our confidence in Him.

surely has a plan. He knows what he is going to do (John 6:6). A wise man said that God does not walk fast, for he is a King. And he is never late, for He is the master of time. It is the idea that he is always on time, with the certainty that he will set before us the missing steps and allow us to progress, once the lesson has been learned.

Return to the Hosting Camp

Let us return to Canapé-Vert at the hosting camp, where we were reflecting on the feasibility to cook for the whole group.

The same scenario of the Bible came to mind. The place was deserted. It was a Port-au-Prince in ruins. Outside, the sight was so terrible, so distressing that we would not even dare to think of being able to find public procurements to buy anything. The rare products saved from the cataclysm were put aside by the storekeepers for the subsistence of their own families or auctioned in the black market.

Then what do we do?

Look how God worked. The church had a program, which aimed at supporting widows in their absolutely essential needs. Every month, the committee responsible organized the stock, the packaging, and the distribution (food pantry). In this way a quantity of reserves was assigned to them on a routine basis, in relation to that assistance.

However, there is more to the story. Indeed, at the beginning of December 2009, the administration had received from Chalè Kreyòl (Haitian ministry in our sister church in Miami) a small cargo of food intended for this group. As we had already stocked up for them for December; the administration decided to resist the temptation to increase their usual quota during the current month and to hold the reserves for January, which usually was called "*the month of the thin cow.*" That is how we had the food in reserve at the beginning of the crisis.

The Twist

The dramatic turn of events in all of this was that the food was in the warehouse, but the people who were in charge of this ministry were not in the camp at that moment. They did not even know that a group had already taken refuge in the premises of the church. We had not contacted them yet because the communication system was completely down. And we at the camp were totally unaware that the food was locked inside.

It was an extraordinary direction of the loyalty of the Lord. How?

The disciples and I who were there present in the camp in Canapé-Vert were working hard in spirit on the possibility of cooking. The focus was for the moment to prepare something at least for the children. The idea of the stored reserve had not even brushed our spirit during our reflections. On the contrary, we were rather concentrated on finding a place where we could buy raw food to cook and drinking water. We even had delegated two brothers ready to leave the camp with the directives to buy everything in their reach without taking into account the rise in prices. We were right in the middle of these reflections, when a sister uttered, "If only we could have something from the widow food program just for today only."

THE POSITION OF THE STORAGE AT THE CHURCH BUILDING

This statement opened our eyes to the possibility of the shipment sent by Chalè Kreyòl from Miami at the beginning of

December. Now we had to verify the hypothesis that something could have still remained from this reserve. It was necessary to see also how we were going to proceed to reach the place where it was probably stored. Certain zones were inaccessible because of the damages. There was as well the risk that the partially destroyed building could totally fall at any time under the influence of the tremors. We had to calculate all these things with good care before venturing out. In the end, we managed to put together all the pieces of the puzzle to reach the warehouse. You can't imagine what we found inside: some big bags of rice, peas, some sugar, some spaghetti, some milk, and some oil sufficient to feed the group during the first seventy-two hours of the crisis. The reserve was discovered by miracle. It was like in a movie. Our eyes opened wide to the loyalty of our God.

We had set out to solve a problem that God Himself had already solved for us. We looked far off from what He had already put down before our feet. Isn't that how God sometimes works? I believe that He had let things happen that way to build our trust and also to make it possible for us to understand the dismay of parents, whom, like us, had been displaced by the earthquake and felt not able to feed their own children on the morning of January 13, 2010. We felt some compassion for their distress. But God knew that this crisis was going to come, and He took care of preparing the necessities for us one month in advance. And I can tell you that from this day of January 13, 2010 to the moment of leaving the hosting camp, we were able to have two warm meals a day.

Isn't God faithful?

The Story of the Tents

Statistics report that the earthquake resulted in 1.3 million homeless persons with approximately 300,000 families living outside

[13]. And we were a part of these statistics. Our first nights were not easy, especially at about two o'clock in the morning. We were all lying in the open-air in the area of the property that seemed to be the most secure. It was necessary for us to be vigilant because the building of the church was half destroyed, was like the sword of Damocles suspended, and could at any time topple under the tugs of the aftershocks. We were lying down by category: the single men together, the sisters together, and the families together. There was not a hint of privacy; we did our best to adapt. God really trained us as a real family. In the night, we could hear the snores of those whose sleep was deeper. It was a distressing situation, especially for the parents who had little children, but we were all welded one to another. The continual exercise of singing, praying, and eating every morning and every evening together moved us closer to each other in unimaginable ways.

The Second Biggest Need

The days passed by quickly, and after the need for food had been satisfied, another most pressing need that we faced was to find tents and blankets. In the meantime, the humanitarian aid from various international organizations began to reach the affected populations. Tents, kits of food, and drinking water had also been distributed. But, it was very difficult to have access to these because of the great demand and stress especially in the first waves of distribution. Even then, God was faithful to us by sending two brothers, one from Montreal and another one from Philadelphia, to help us to overcome this difficulty in finding tents. I remember the moment they told me, one morning when leaving the camp to go and make the initial search, "Pray. We are going to establish contacts to see how we could find tents for the camp."

Two hours later, we received a message asking us to send a small van to an address to receive tents. With God, it does not take time for our problems to be resolved; it is done as soon as He wants it. All that count is that we are on His side.

When the LORD takes pleasure in anyone's way, he causes their enemies to make peace with them. (Proverbs 16:7)

Transformed into a City

When tents arrived in the hosting camp, all the faces shone with enjoyment. The caterpillar that transformed into an attractive butterfly is a good illustration of the change that occurred within the hosting camp. After the distribution of tents, followed by their installation, the camp became a real city, all new. I can still see the joy that shone on the children's faces. They went back and forth from one tent to another, claiming each to have the most beautiful one. It was a big thing for them. We were all satisfied to be able to sleep now in the warmth. The enormous privilege was offered to us to be counted among the first ones served in this context of big pressure. Thanks to God in the first place, and thank you also to these two brothers who took steps to help us to solve this crucial problem.

From the Lodging Camp to the Village

Let us consider that all which was made there from the beginning of the crisis was as the cherry on top of the cake. And the cake itself was the village conceived and built for the relocation of the people of the camps. It was this last action that crowned all others already taken during the whole time of the camp. Besides the fact that we were able to eat, receive tents, find psychological support, have access to a professional program where people were trained, so that they would be able to fly by themselves when the time would have come, to top all that, in cooperation with the management of Hope Haiti and Hope Worldwide, we decided also to work on a more sustainable plan that would contribute to the stability of families in the long run. And the idea of the village blossomed and subsequently materialized.

When God wants to bless, He does not do it halfway. He is faithful, and his loyalty exceeds our capacity to understand it.

To Him alone be the glory!

CHAPTER 4

THE LIGHTNING

THE LIGHTNING

"Why, you do not even know what will happen tomorrow. What is your life? You are a mist that appears for a little while and then vanishes" (James 4:14).

This passage of the Bible accentuates the brevity of life. Life is compared with a mist which quickly fades. Moses is right when he says in his prayer of Psalm 90: *"Teach us to number our days that we may gain a heart of wisdom."*

Without pretending to its complete sense this statement of the prophet would mean: Teach us to be conscious of the fact that we are not here for too long. So every day should be lived as if it were our last.

Another reflection on the brevity of life is the fact that we have limitations on our means of control. Nowadays, the scientists have made major revolutionary advances in technology by creating a series of machines, which detect almost everything. Let us consider for example, the GPS (Global Positioning System) that, by merely indicating the address of the destination, allows us to go from one point to another one without having the slightest idea of the road to be followed. It is good to enjoy these extraordinary discoveries. Some of these machines are even strategically installed by some of the most advanced countries. Others are designed to detect metals and narcotics forbidden in zones such as in airports. Think of the big advances in the medical sector, which are largely due to scientific and technological progress realized during the twentieth century. Thus, there is no doubt that miracles are made by human beings by tools which they handle with incomparable dexterity. However, as creative as we are, we can never invent the machine capable of reading us the exact date, the place, and the circumstances of our own deaths. This is an exclusive attribute of God's wisdom to which He alone holds the key. The event of the earthquake crystallized this biblical assertion very well.

Human Frailty

There were at least about 230,000 souls who perished during this cataclysm in Haiti. But, shouldn't we also mention of those who get killed every day in other ways, such as in road accidents, drowning, or from the many diseases that are devastating the human race?

We are beautiful creatures made in the image of God; it couldn't happen any other way. However, we also have to admit that our fragility is proportional to our beauty. No eyewitness would have hesitated to ask himself the question, *"What is man?"* as he watched the spectacle in the streets of Port-au-Prince on the morning of January 13, 2010. The number of casualties was enormous, and the city did not have enough funeral homes to help in the management of so many deaths. The authorities had to ask the population to come take their corpses and place them by the roadside. From there, they were to be removed and transported to Titayen, where a mass grave was created for that purpose. There were no last tributes planned for the dead, according to the rules of our customary funeral ceremonies. It was very heartbreaking to see dead bodies covered with white sheets stacked up by the roadside. They were intended to be picked up by the public roads service, as when trashcans are put outside for collection by the district, but what other choice did the authorities have? It was the most suitable solution to prevent the decomposition of the corpses and to protect the survivors from infection, which would have by far complicated the situation.

Very Close to the Finish Line

I can imagine that morning of January 12, 2010, as people left their houses to go to the office, to school, or to other personal activities. They greeted their loved ones goodbye, with the hope to see them again that evening. I do not think that they had scheduled in their plans to not return home. Some of them had agendas filled with activities to be carried out, according to their dreams: a family to take care of, studies to finish, and projects to finalize. Nevertheless, they were very close to their finish lines. In this battle, we need to consider that death has no horn. We may be or have what we want, but for each of us a fate is drawn: scholars or illiterates, rich or poor, white or black, young or old—there is nothing we can do to avoid being caught by the reaper.

It is only a matter of time. Oh, how vulnerable we are!

Let's Embrace Wisdom

Living with wisdom would be the best alternative one could offer themselves during their pilgrimage before facing death. Conscious of our vulnerability, wisdom would want us to grab hold of the most important things in life: those that relate to our relationship with God and our relationship with others. These two things are indispensable. The Bible says *All the Law and the Prophets hang on these two commandments* (Matthew 22:40).

Personal Relationship with God

Here is what our world needs today. Any real wisdom begins by initiating a personal relationship with God. Why? Paul gave a very good reason to the Colossians on this:

> Since, then, you have been raised with Christ, set your hearts on things above, where Christ is, seated at the right hand of God. Set your minds on things above, not on earthly things. For you died, and your life is now hidden with Christ in God. (Colossians 3:1–4)

During our time here on the earth, everybody should make sure that their life is hidden with Christ in God. The life hidden with Christ is like a credit card that the bank gives you to allow you to make your transactions without any cash. It is the same thing from the spiritual point of view. When we have our life hidden with Christ, we have the credit that is all settled when it comes to death. Whether it comes in the morning, at noon, or in the evening, we don't worry because it is all settled in advance.

Have you already done what's necessary to have your life be hidden with Jesus?

To have your life hidden with Christ:

1. You have to hear the Word of God

Anyone who wants to start a personal relationship with God must hear God's Word. It is the first step on the staircase that leads to faith (*Romans 10:17*).

2. You have to believe in the Word of God

It is not enough to only read the Bible and to do Bible studies; you must also decide to believe in the living Word and to take God seriously. This is the second step (*Hebrews 11:6*).

3. You must repent

You have to repent. That means we demonstrate our faith by no longer doing the things that are forbidden by God. At the same time, we begin to put into practice the things that God calls us to do. This is the third step (*Luke 13:3*).

4. Confess Jesus as Lord

We have to publicly confess that Jesus is Lord, and from then on, we stop being our own lord and master. This is the fourth step (*Romans 10:9*).

5. Be baptized

Be baptized for the forgiveness of your sins. This is where the new creation begins. The Holy Spirit is given as a gift, and the life of the person is hidden with Jesus in God. This is the fifth step (*Acts 2:38*).

6. Perseverance

Persevere until we die (*Hebrews 10:35–36*).

Here, we just gave you a little hand to help you know what to do if you intend to have a relationship with God. This is the biblical process to become a Christian. All other formulas are incompatible with biblical teachings.

Work on Your Relationship with Others

From the onset, we have to agree to the fact that this is not an easy exercise. Why not? Because there is an ocean full of differences between people. God has created us to be unique, each one of us. The psalmist David said, *I praise you because I am fearfully and wonderfully made; your works are wonderful, I know that full well (Psalm 139:14).*

Our peculiarities don't only come from the shape of our faces, the color of our skin, or our fingerprints, but they also reflect our character and our tastes. Every person is a work of art, drawn and signed by God. Thus there are as many tastes and characters as individuals living on the planet (approximately 7.3 billion). The Big Architect's creativity is unlimited.

To Live Together

We are created differently, but we are called to live in a community. So, when it comes to putting all of who we are in a single basket, our strengths or weaknesses, our shortcomings or attributes, and to find the happy medium, which would give a minimum of satisfaction to everyone in the basket becomes an exercise that requires an amount of patience and even of tolerance, that often we do not naturally have in our spiritual account.

In the previous chapter, I mentioned that God had trained us to really feel like a family (speaking of the people who attended the accommodation camp). In the camp, we were not only there for Sunday service or that of the midweek, where hugs and beautiful smiles are exchanged. This time, instead of short durations of time, we were tied together for almost two years in that adventure. We saw each other in the morning, noon, and evening. All our weaknesses of character were exposed in broad daylight. Nobody would have been able to put on a mask twenty-four hours a day, without his or her real personality not being revealed. We were taking, directly, a whole series of lessons around tolerance.

Yes, we loved each other. Yes, we sang and prayed together, but we cannot deny that there always were also conflicts to be managed—disputes bound to our differences in points of view and feelings. It is generally in this fateful crossroads of living together that division takes shape and then settles down at every level of society today. Even marriages exemplify this. According to figures, there are approximately 876,000 cases of divorce annually in the United States. We know very well that this is not a wound of America only but of the whole planet. A lot of partners, as cordial as was their professional relationship at first, eventually part ways—and sometimes with an unpleasant note—ending their experience of working together. A quick look also allows us to see how many countries are at war in the world. Most of them are as a result of fratricide. Others are wars of state, which diplomacy was not able to prevent and contain.

The Déchouquage

In Haiti, there is a phenomenon called "*déchouquage*," which was started after the fall of Duvalier in 1986. It is a form of violence that first aimed at the members of the body of volunteers of the National Security (V.N.S). They were better known under the name of Tontons macoutes. The role of this paramilitary body was to ensure the security of the Duvalier regime. The houses of these volunteers were ransacked and or destroyed by groups of people. They themselves were beaten or killed if they were not rescued by the police. Since 1986, the déchouquage was maybe modernized, by taking other forms and aimed at other individuals, but it lives on no less as real, as so many in the last thirty years have come to know humiliation, beatings, unjust dismissal, and even death.

Why? Simply because the spirit of dialogue and forthrightness were substituted by this infernal instrument that is the déchouquage. Marek Halter said with good reason that *"Violence starts where speech stops."*[14] But whether you call it divorce, war, déchouquage, separation, or division between individuals, spouses, partners, or even nations only has at its root in pride and selfishness.

How to Overcome This Gangrene That Plagues the World?

The Bible gives us a cluster of directives, which contain some elements of prevention and restoration.

The first element of prevention — *Humility.*

In the epistle of the apostle Paul to the Philippians, 2:3–5, the Bible reads *Rather, in humility value others above yourselves.*

By virtue of this spiritual principle, we are supposed to consider others as if they were above us. This scripture does not say that we are inferior to them. It is not an invitation to cheat yourself either. It is rather an attitude of heart that God urges us to develop so that we do not try to elevate ourselves above others. This spiritual virtue prevents conflict. It clearly goes against human perception because, very often instead of seeing others as being above ourselves, we wait on the contrary for others to look at us with that eye. We want to be known by all as the strongest, the most talented, the wealthiest, and the most *"everything"* — as long as it is praiseworthy. That is an attitude that seems registered in our human genes and keeps us in the logic of open or concealed rivalry. But, by considering ourselves lower with all that we are or have, the other would be better predisposed to walk by our side in an atmosphere of friendliness and trust. That attitude would provoke in him or her the feeling of embarking, not on the dynamics of a leading-subjugated relationship, but rather one that of a real partnership characterized by mutual respect.

If your relationship with others is plummeting, check and see if the problem is not at that level.

And let's try humility!

The second element of prevention—*Altruism*.

Not looking to your own interests but each of you to the interests of the others (Philippians 2:4). The lack of trust that affects relationships comes, to a certain extent, from the fact that in these relationships, each one has to fight as in a bullring to hold its own to assert their own interests. It is purely a selfish circle, where there is always a sort of suspicion.

In his book, *Overcoming Hurts and Anger*, Dwight Carlson, MD writes,

> *We all tend to have myopia; that is, we are focused on our own little world—our needs, feelings, and wishes. We seldom give even equal attention to another person's perspective, trying to see the world through their eyes. [15]*

Carlson's declaration cannot be fairer than that. Imagine what the world would be like if in our conjugal or friendly, professional or diplomatic relations, the interest of the other party would also have been taken into account just as ours. Our society would be a much better place. Certain conflicts would vanish automatically, and trust would reign over distrust.

Consider also that the interest of others is one of the keys that opens doors to cordiality and sincerity of relationships. In all our exchanges, we learn to go above and beyond by putting ourselves in the other person's shoes and to consider their understanding around the common situation. From then on, we will be able to give correct answers with the appropriate attitude and without compromise. This type of parley creates a win-win instead of the win-lose situation that often leads to cold war.

You may be saying to yourself, why should I do it this way? Jorel, you don't know who I am dealing with. You do not understand.

Look, if the circumstances are difficult and you still choose to do what God calls you to do, that will show God that you really trust Him. And as He sees and controls everything, He will take your faith into account.

The Example of Abraham

The story of Abraham in the Bible (Genesis 13) provides an example for us to study. Here we pick up on the conflict between the shepherds of Lot and those of Abraham. Abraham knew very well that his nephew was no angel and that he would dare to make this deal. So he said to Lot:

> Let's not have any quarreling between you and me, or between your herders and mine, for we are close relatives. Is not the whole land before you? Let's part company. If you go to the left, I'll go to the right; if you go to the right, I'll go to the left. (Genesis 13: 8–9)

By giving Lot the first choice, it was the window that the uncle opened for him to prove himself forthcoming. Abraham did not give Lot the benefit of deciding for him: the verdict of the choice that he would have made, the attitude of heart to be adopted in this situation. Abraham had already taken his own position even before talking to Lot. What position, you ask? That of giving him the first choice and remaining at peace with his nephew and also preventing the division between their servants.

Because of that, we see him acting as if he was weak. He did not claim his seniority rights and demand the most fertile part for himself. He did not even take the 50–50 compromise option. I do not think that it would have been a bad approach for him because nobody would feel put out at the end of the negotiations. However, Abraham simply decided to go farther by inviting him to choose the part that he preferred. So, the father of nations defused the potential explosives resting in the heart of his nephew, even in the case where he would be a conflicting character.

Keeping peace with others may sometimes be only the result of a firm determination. Denial of self and humility are needed. Here in this story, Abraham's biggest victory does not come because an amicable solution with Lot was found, but because he was rather able to maintain the purity of his heart toward his nephew in the following days. He had no place either for hostility or resentment. Later when Lot was in danger where he had settled, we see the uncle urgently mobilizing his servants to help him. What an example of spirituality! Would you do all this for a nephew who had not shown consideration for you in the past?

That is what the father of faith has crystallized: sensitivity, patience, love, and wisdom in his relationships with others. His trust in God was his only motive to act this way. This is what you and I must imitate to please God.

First element of restoration—*Resolution of conflicts*

If your brother or sister sins go and point out their fault, just between the two of you. If they listen to you, you have won them over. But if they will not listen, take one or two others along, so that 'every matter may be established by the testimony of two or three witnesses.' If they still refuse to listen, tell it to the church; and if they refuse to listen even to the church, treat them as you would a pagan or a tax collector. (Matthew 18: 15–17)

We saw through Abraham the preventive effect of humility and altruism in his relationship with others. However, this spiritual virtue, although practiced by some, does not eradicate conflict for all humanity. From the smallest social cell, which is the family, to the most complex ethnic group, conflict is always present. As sinners, it is impossible that there are no conflicts between us, and no mechanism of human prevention can be effective enough for us to avoid them completely. The challenge belongs to us to grow up in the art of solving conflict and to restore our relationships when they are damaged.

In this word of Jesus in the gospel of Matthew, we learn to speak directly to the concerned person. If she/he listens to you, the case is closed. But, if she/he does not listen to you, you pursue peace by appealing to others capable of helping. In the case that the situation is not yet solved, we bring him/her to the church until the problem is completely eradicated.

Note: For a conflict to be resolved fast and in an effective manner, the parties should decide to approach it with spiritual weapons.

Some elements that can help:

a. We do our best to follow the steps mentioned by Jesus in the Gospel to avoid the slander and the belittlement. Because, when conflict resolution is not done well, things can worsen instead of being resolved.

b. We have to remain righteous by putting things into perspective and looking for a solution. Even in a situation of conflict, God may be glorified. And one of the ways to do this is not to try to be right at all costs, but to be quick to recognize our own faults, own them, and change. This is what really matters.

c. Another important element comes from the way to restore the other at fault. A scripture complementary to Matthew 18, still in the context of resolving conflicts, is found in Galatians 6:1–2:

> Brothers and sisters, if someone is caught in a sin, you who live by the Spirit should restore that person gently. But watch yourselves, or you also may be tempted. Carry each other's burdens, and in this way you will fulfill the law of Christ.

The first step to resolve conflict is to speak to your counterpart, but the big question is to know how to approach this. Galatians gives us the directive: *restore that person gently.* The majority of cases show absence of this ingredient complicates the outcome. We cannot resolve a conflict if our hearts are filled with anger and passion. I admit that it is difficult when feeling hurt or betrayed to still find the capacity to be soft.

Let us see what Proverbs 25:15 tells us: *Through patience a ruler can be persuaded, and a gentle tongue can break a bone.* Thus, this is not about the anger which we spew out in an attempt to force the other person to admit fault or speaking in a disrespectful tone, thinking this will move the person's heart and lead to the expected result. Of course, we have the right to get angry in the face of mediocrity, but also we have the duty not to be controlled by anger.

Again, in his book *Overcoming Hurts and Anger*, Dwight Carlson gives a great illustration to show the attitude that would be conceivable when it comes to anger. He said:

> Anger is like a fire in a fireplace in a remote cabin during a blizzard. If the fire gets out of control it will destroy the occupants, either directly by burning them up, or indirectly by forcing them to flee and die of exposure in the blizzard. On the other hand, if the fire goes out, they will freeze even though they are in the cabin. The key, then, is adequate respect for and control of the fire. [16]

I do not know how many times in my life I have failed having the right control of the fire. But one experience helped me to see things more clearly and to grow. In 1998, I was leading the church in Cap-Haitian. As young pastor, full of zeal, I was working with the church to help every member come to service on time. But a certain brother with whom I had already spoken with two or three times about this continued to come late. One day, I was annoyed about his continued tardiness, so I decided to confront him because he lived closer to where we meet than any other member of the church.

At that time in our church in Haiti, we tended to speak in radical terms, and the notion of being radical was soiled by a stereotype. To be radical meant being strict with others when they were not doing right. Many of us of that generation in the church wanted to build this image of being radical. As a result, some of our challenges tended to be more forceful than sympathetic, more hurtful than healing. In certain cases, patience and compassion were seen as a sign of shrouded weakness and even as cowardice. Oftentimes, without meaning to, because of our lack of wisdom, we failed in the delicate task of preserving the sinner while helping him/her to deal with his/her sins.

Well, I told myself that I was going to be very radical with this brother in regard to his attitude, but I can tell you that that time turned into a catastrophe. The problem was not the fact that I met him alone or even that I wanted to confront somebody who was rebellious. It was more in the way that I approached the situation, following the logic of that radicalness described previously. Things turned out very worldly. I had hurt him instead of helping him see his sin and to repent. This brother had become very aggressive to the point that I was afraid. I can tell you that if I had not left, who knows what would have happened.

The following morning, while meditating on the situation of the day before, I realized that I too had sinned by taking it personally. I was not gentle; I had raised my voice. I wanted to help this brother change, but the weapon I used was carnal. Thus, it turned out bad. I was aware of my responsibility, so I had scheduled another meeting with him to apologize for not having respected him and to face the issue with a better attitude. And the good news is that my repentance had helped him make a lot of changes.

The lesson learned: Carnal weapons should never be used to solve spiritual problems.

> For our struggle is not against flesh and blood, but against the rulers, against the authorities, against the powers of this dark world and against the spiritual forces of evil in the heavenly realms. Therefore put on the full armor of God, so that when the day of evil comes, you may be able to stand your ground, and after you have done everything, to stand. (Ephesians 6:12–13)

In meetings like these, an open Bible and prayer should always be included for the best outcome. Otherwise, you risk being run

95

out of the home like the brothers of Sceva in Acts 19, not in a physical way, but in an emotional and spiritual way.

I believe that people who are invested with authority should pay attention to how they address the faults of their subordinates. Men should think about how they address their wives or their children, especially in the tone and attitude when they are irritated. Sometimes we are more capable of being the leader than of being the affectionate husband, the patient father, or the friendly boss. And this, not to create comfortable and fluid relationships, is rather to raise invisible walls, however real.

This point is directed primarily to those in authority and to men in general because they are chosen by God to serve—by example—as guides to society. However, it is also imperative that, in return, they receive from the other elements of the chain, the respect and submission that are due to them. It is a two-way street, and they are not always at fault.

Get rid of our long-standing conflicts once and for all and eradicate them by applying the guidelines that God gives us throughout the Bible and adopting the attitude he shows us. Time does not erase our unresolved conflicts; it exacerbates them.

The second element of restoration—*Forgiveness*

For if you forgive other people when they sin against you, your heavenly Father will also forgive you. But if you do not forgive others their sins, your Father will not forgive your sins (Matthew 6 14–15). This scripture hurts us in the heart, as a scalpel, because it challenges us to do one of the most difficult spiritual exercises of Christianity. Sometimes we even ignore whether we know how to forgive or not because the profound meaning of this word is not well captured. Nevertheless, it is a very important step in the management of conflicts. We can, within the framework of resolution of a dispute, spend hours talking to each other. Each party can accept its share of responsibility for the problem. Words of apology may even be exchanged. But what will make all these initiatives work toward real reconciliation is a small word of three syllables called "FOR-GIVE-NESS." It is that word that will recover any injury in our relationships after healing them.

What Are the Signs of Real Forgiveness?

The word *forgiveness* is the equivalent of the Greek word "*apheimi*" which means: remove, payoff a debt, let go. We know that we have really forgiven if we accept the payoff from the other person for the debt for the offense. Just like when we put a seal on a document to validate it, this is what forgiveness represents in the resolution of a conflict. It is offered to the other person to mean that we have erased his/her offense. Do you think that it is easy? No! It takes surpassing oneself, but especially a strong dose of the will of a heart to please God. We all want to be able to forgive because we all want to also be forgiven by the Lord. What is lacking in us is often our capacity to get there. I do not believe that there is a specific method to follow to get there. What is for certain is that the closer we are to God, the less difficult it will be for us to decide to forgive and to stick to it.

Some humble advice

1. Strengthen the muscles of your heart spiritually

The heart is the most important organ in the accomplishment of certain exercises whether physical or spiritual. In big sporting events, like the Olympics for example, the performance of the athletes is directly connected to the health of their heart. Even before engaging in certain disciplines, athletes have the responsibility of consulting their cardiologist for an evaluation of their heart. Depending on the diagnosis, the athletes can be recommended to pursue their goal or to solve their cardiac pathologies prior to venturing into such endeavors.

It is the same approach in the spiritual point of view. There are some exercises that are not easy to do if the heart is not in good shape. One of them is to be able to forgive when we are hurt. This process requires a sum of spiritual energy that only a strong heart can produce. We can have good intentions, but it is not enough to succeed. In these crossroads, I profoundly believe that only the Word of God is capable of disciplining our

> Just like when we put a seal on a document to validate it, this is what forgiveness represents in the resolution of a conflict. It is offered to the other person to mean that we have erased his offense.

hearts to bring forgiveness (Hebrews 4:12–13). Do some character studies like Joseph and Jesus, so that you may be able to imitate their example. Read these scriptures several times. Copy them. Hold the essential fragments until they penetrate your heart. The first battle to win is definitively the one to have a heart predisposed to forgiveness.

2. Protect your heart against bad thoughts

From my youngest spiritual age, I learned that it was important to protect our heart against all that could poison it. We pay attention to the audiovisual scenes susceptible to cause bad thoughts. We don't hesitate to close our eyes in front of a vulgar screen in the theater. We change the channel of the television to avoid a scandalous scene. We look for another station on the radio to avoid listening to the unwholesome lyrics of a song. We do all this to give ourselves a chance to stay on the right track. Nevertheless, we often fail by missing the target, but we make this effort daily with the unique goal of protecting our hearts.

I believe it is also a good exercise to try if we want to make it through forgiveness. This is because if we continue to nurture in our heart or to brood in our spirit scenes that weaken our heart, how can we expect our initial decision to forgive to also not be weakened? It's true that negative and dark thoughts are going to invade your mind to remove the spirit of forgiveness, but chase them away with positive thoughts like: *"Father, forgive me as I also forgive those who offended me with their thought of hurting me, but God changed evil for good."*

Why do you think people continue to be so angry for situations that date as far back as five or ten years? Why do you think that their hurt remains so great, even after all this time, like it was yesterday that they had been hurt?

The answer is simple; they have not changed the channel of the TV nor closed their eyes when they needed to keep out negative thoughts. If the battle is not won at the thought level, we risk being caught subtly by hostility. And our efforts for peace will not be crowned in spite of our good intentions.

3. Pray for victory

As sinners, we are incapable of forgiving when we are hurt. It is beyond our human capacity. If it was easy, there would be much less hostility. Families would be more united. Relationships in the church would be less superficial. Forgiveness is a spiritual discipline that requires a lot of self-denial. And the level of self-denial varies according to the type, the nature, and the depth of the relationship that binds us together. The closer we were to the offender, the more devastating will the offense prove to be. Therefore, more difficult it will also be to trust again. However, it should also be noted that our love for people is not measured solely on what we say or offer, but also takes into account the sum of the debt that we are prepared to cancel for them when they hurt us in doing wrong. Love and the spirit of forgiveness go hand in hand.

The Bible tells us: *"Be perfect, therefore, as your heavenly Father is perfect"* (Matthew 5:48).

The Peasant's Garden

When I think about forgiveness, I remember a lesson that the young peasant must learn to have a good crop, in using fertilizer as a supplement. The first lesson consists in learning how to place the fertilizer (the urea) down and around seeds. If the nitrogen is sowed haphazardly, it will have no impact on the development of the seed. The second lesson is to respect the distance in which the chemical must be put down with regard to the seed (5 or 15 cm depending on the dose and that varies depending on the size of the garden). Otherwise the roots risk being burned.

Practical Points

The desire to forgive is like a seed that we plant—the seed of forgiveness. Burying the offense is the fertilizer which, by burying it, forgiveness may grow. It is here the idea of planting both with the hope that one, by dying, is going to serve as fertilizer for the other to grow. It is up to us to plead specifically in our prayers to be able to place the offense at the right distance, meaning being able to gradually forget it. It is only at this price that the seed of our forgiveness may sprout, grow, and produce the fruit of purity and acceptance for the benefit of the offender.

And if getting through this task seems too tough for us, why not seek the support of someone we trust? From then on, when

God visits us, he will find forgiveness instead of resentment and love instead of hatred. The burden, once deposited, will make us lighter. However, what will especially make us happy is to have accomplished an act that is so difficult, but which pleases our Master.

Why fight for our relationship with God and with others?

Although you have just pondered with me on the necessity of working out our relationship with God and with others, now it is important to understand—why? *Pi bonè se granm maten*, a Haitian proverb, tells us this. It simply means "The sooner, the better."

I had a final exam in my English class that took place in a big room equipped for these kinds of tests. When you arrive at the place, they give you a paper that contains a reference number and a password. The reference number assigns you to a well-isolated booth and the password gives you access to the computer prepared in the booth for that purpose. The test consisted of three parts: a vocabulary test, an oral exam, and an essay test. We had sixty minutes to complete the work.

To pass an exam like that, you had to prepare yourself. The secret laid in the following two words: fast and well. The first experience was more difficult because I did not expect to have the test in this format. It was the first time in my life that I was going to take a test on a computer. I did not know of this in advance. I would have taken at least a few nights to train myself, to crop my fingers if I'd known. But, the most stressful thing was when the system indicated I had fifteen minutes left of the regular time.

What! I sighed.

Imagine someone taking an exam in a foreign language who had not mastered basic typing techniques too well. Fortunately, the computer keyboard does not make much noise like the keyboards of typewriters of the '80s; otherwise they would probably have asked me to leave the room to take the test alone. Moving on!

The Element of Surprise

Knowing that I did not have a lot of time, I was doing my best to finish my work and suddenly, when I reached the conclusion of my essay, the computer automatically shut down. My time was then consumed. *"Wow! The sixty minutes go too fast,"* I thought. The same disappointment could also be read on the faces of all the other students who had not, like me, finished the exam. There is nothing more regrettable to not have finished what we ought and could just because of time.

Shouldn't life be considered like an hour exam? It goes fast like lightning; too fast, as some people would say. Moses tells us in Psalm 90:10, *Our days may come to seventy years, or eighty, if our strength endures.*

Life is short. Consequently, shouldn't we focus on the essential things to keep it simple? In pursuing many things, we often miss those that matter the most. For a journey so ephemeral, why not make the effort to reduce the distance that separates us from our family, our parents, and our friends? That would be a good starting point. I am not talking about the distance that is measured in miles. It often turns out that two people who live on two ends of the world are closer than two others who live under the same roof. It is about the distance that has to do with our emotional connection with others. That is one of the biggest lessons that I personally learned through the tragedy of January 12, 2010.

Indeed, I was not with my family on the passage of the earthquake. And when I went back home, seeing the barrier blocked, and the house shaken without any sign of life coming to me from inside, I became really distressed in thinking they were killed. But, my pain was relieved when I learned that the family was fortunately safe. I quickly rushed to the public square where thousands of people had taken refuge, and that is where I found my squad. Taking them into my arms, I felt that they had become dearer to me than before. So, I realized how important it is for someone to seize the opportunity that God gives them to be present alongside those we love, to cherish and serve them. This tragedy shows that nobody knows which one of those hugs, kisses, or admiring glances will be kept, at the end of the day, as the last one.

Another Fact

It should be emphasized that in the exam room, as soon as your time ran out, the computer would shut down by itself. Whether you are finished or not, it shuts down. You cannot ask for a few additional minutes to finish the exam. The system has no ears to listen to our complaints, nor a heart to empathize with us. It's a machine that executes the command for which it was programmed. It will not shut down one minute before, just as it will not allow a minute more.

Isn't that like the face of death?

It's been two years since one of my best friends, my father in the faith, died young after having succumbed to a brutal kind of cancer. It was a hard blow, considering what he represented for the church in Haiti, my family, and me in particular. I admit that it would have been a more terrible blow if we had not been sure of his final destiny with God. We have lost several of our loved ones in the same way with a feeling of powerlessness for not being able to do anything to keep them with us.

It is death!

The same evening of the earthquake, a young brother in the faith arrived on the church's property, part of the first ten to arrive. Still, under the shock of what he had lived, he explained to us that he was on the street for the first big jolt, thinking that it was the end of the world, so he wanted to make it to the church's location. Why? He thought if he was going to die, he wanted to die at the usual place of worship. It was a beautiful thought to tell you the truth, but it lacked maturity. We don't need a specific address for death to come find us.

> We don't need a specific address for death to come find us. But, when it grabs us, we must have the address where we want it to take us. After all, our guarantee is only sealed on what our destination is, regarding the life choices that we have made and not by the place where it finds us.

But when it grabs us, we must have the address where we want it to take us. After all, our guarantee is only sealed on what our destination is, regarding the life choices that we have made and not by the place where it finds us. The main thing is to realize that time is short, and we must be eager to do good in order to be ready for our last appointment regardless of the hour and the place—all before the system ends our pilgrimage.

Don't spend all your time pursuing career, power, and money without making enough time for God and for others. When we leave this earth, we have to make sure we are in good terms with God and with our fellow men; therein lie the essential things of life.

Think about it! And make decisions.

CHAPTER 5

THE RELOCATION

THE RELOCATION

Life in the Accommodation Camp

The time spent at the accommodation camp was in many ways a spiritual learning center for us who stayed there. In the chapter on "The Lightning," I spoke of the lessons on the spirit of tolerance that we have learned in order to live together, sharing the same space. But, there were so many more. We went through several stages, and each step brought to us a lot of lessons. Here are some of them:

1. The simplicity

Although owning a tent in the middle of the 2010 crisis in Haiti was a considerable privilege, after several hundred days in the tent, one was able to raise some disadvantages related to this type of accommodation. First of all, we have to understand that there is a huge difference between staying in a tent for a picnic day or a religious activity like a retreat, for example, and living in a tent for months as part of a humanitarian crisis.

When it is for recreational or spiritual purposes for a short time, everyone can feel enthusiastic about this adventure, where life is reduced to its simplest expression. Nothing can be complicated in a tent. No furniture, no domestic appliance—just the strict minimum: our sleeping bags, blankets, clothes, shoes, toiletries and boys' school bags in my case. But when the counter starts to go over weeks and from weeks to months, you start then to have the real taste of what it means to live in a camp. It's easy, at this point, to lose your gratefulness if you are not connected to God.

The great lesson of the simplicity starts with the size of the occupied tent, which varied between three and twelve square meters depending on the size of your family. I was among those who had a big dimension. From a house of three bedrooms, we were called by the circumstances to accommodate ourselves in a space which was a little bit bigger than one of our two bathrooms. The management of this plastic cage for a family of four required military discipline. Despite bringing in only what was necessary, there was not enough space to stretch out. It appeared sometimes more difficult to manage this twelve square meters than a large house. The more stuff that had been introduced inside, the more complicated it became to manage it. There was no choice; we had to adjust ourselves to a simple lifestyle. Still today, even though different changes had been in operation during those seven to eight years after the disaster, when I think about the tent that we occupied, the picture that comes to mind is the image of a pan—the pan of simplicity.

We really had learned how to live there with very little.

2. The patience and self-control

In the camp, we did not have enough sanitary facilities for the group. We had only two toilets: one allocated to women and the other to men. We were facing the constraint of the toilet queue, especially before and after our worship services. So, in the hours before the services, you really had to wait to take a shower or give up. And the test came up when some of us took much more time than what was usually allowed to anyone. After the meetings, the same queue was sometimes observed, with much more demand. Sunday services were not only for Christians in the accommodation camp, but also for those in the downtown area. When everyone met, there's no need to detail the pressure that was put on the two available sanitary facilities. And the trickiest thing in this queuing question was that, sometimes, the needs were not always returnable like the bath before worship. We took those two classes at the same time (patience and self-control). And at the end of the session, when we left the camp, I can tell you some of us had graduated in getting our master's degree in these aspects. How? We had really learned how to wait under pressure.

3. The appreciation

In John 2:1–10 we read the following:

> Three days later there was a wedding at Cana in Galilee. Jesus' mother was there and Jesus was also invited to the wedding with his disciples. The wine having finished, the mother said to him: they have no more wine. Jesus answered her, "Woman, what is there between you and me? My hour has not yet come. His mother said to the servants, "Do whatever he tells you." Now there were six stone vessels for the purification of the Jews, each containing two or three measures. Jesus said to them, Fill these vessels with water. And they filled them to the brim. Now draw, "he said," and carry it to the overseer of the meal. "And they carried it. When the ruler of the meal had tasted the water changed into wine, not knowing where the wine came from, while the servants who had drawn water knew it well — he called the bridegroom and said to him: "every man is first used

to good wine, then not so good once he is drunk; You
have kept the good wine until now."

In this story, the wedding of Cana reported by John's gospel,
the organizer soon appreciated the wine that Jesus miracu-
lously made from water because he had tasted the first wine.
He described it as inferior, in comparison of that offered by
Jesus during this event. If the authorizer of the meal for some
reason had not had a drink of the first wine, how would he
have been able to enjoy the new wine and express himself on
the difference between the two flavors? He would perhaps be
capable of assuming, under the testimony of others, that the
wine of Jesus was much better. But, there would be no personal
and legitimate testimony. In this regard, it is crucial to understand that God leaves us sometimes in a difficult situation for
a while to prepare ourselves and sharpen our appreciation for
what He will provide for us later. As I mentioned earlier, we
were called to appreciate the different marches that we had by
the grace of God in the process of relocation. In other words,
we would not have sufficiently appreciated the tents that we got
if we had not experienced sleeping outside with our kids for a
while. Only those who know how challenging it is to stay in a
tent for months can appreciate the improved shelters that God
granted to the village.

The Story of the Toothbrush

On the morning of January 13, as I woke up in the church's yard,
I felt the need to brush my teeth before doing anything else, as
usual. Oops! Unfortunately, I did not have my toothbrush. And
this time, I could not ask Junie if she had seen it for me. I knew
it was stuck inside the house. Throughout the morning, while
working with others on the mechanism that was going to help
manage the camp for the survivors, I became more and more
uncomfortable with that unpleasant sleeping taste in my mouth.

However, I had to deny myself. It was such a minute detail in light of the situation. Besides, it would be absurd and even improper to mention that I missed my toothbrush, while others around me were missing their loved ones. At times, I thought of using my forefinger, but with what toothpaste? That morning, inside of me, I became aware that there was a detail missing—a bit of toothpaste on a brush and then a cup of coffee. And that was the beginning of a new lifestyle. I realized how blessed we are sometimes with little things that we don't even consider, as if they do not exist, until the day they are taken from us. Ever since that time, I began to consider the need to appreciate even the little things that I am blessed with, instead of complaining about things that—even with good reason—I would need.

> I believe there will always be, at least, one reason for a person to either be thankful for what she/he has or to complain about what she/he desires. The choice will often depend on our perspectives. Once we find this reason, we can better determine which side we want to join: those who are bitter or those who remain positive.

I would like to end this section by saying that I'm a very blessed man. I'm very grateful that we came through and are physically intact when, sadly, as a result of the earthquake, a multitude of people were left orphaned, without their loved ones, or without a limb. I'm very thankful that by the grace of God, I became a disciple of Jesus Christ. I have a virtuous wife. I have two handsome and wonderful boys. I also have extraordinary friends around the world. In addition, I have the hope of eternal life. These are the things that I keep in mind and that keep me encouraged in sunny days or cloudy ones. Thus, I came to believe that there will always be at least one reason for a person to either be thankful for what she/he has or to complain about what she/he desires. The choice will often depend on our perspectives. Once we find this reason, we can better determine which side we want to join: those who are bitter or those who remain positive.

FROM THE HOSTING CAMP TO THE VILLAGE.

THE THREE MAIN STEPS IN THE TRANSITION

A. OUTDOOR NIGHTS. B. ACCESS TO TENTS. C. LIVING IN A HOUSE.

Life in the Village

FAMILIES HAVE FINALLY REACHED THE VILLAGE

View of a closed-up unit in the village after years of accommodation

The Portrait of the Village

The village is built on a total area of 12,900 square meters. There are forty-four residences, a church building, a clinic building, and a playground. There is also a filtration system with a hydraulic pump for the purification of drinking water as well as many other infrastructures to improve the quality of life there.

The Portrait of a House

Each house has a well distributed area of fifty-two square meters. It is composed of two large rooms, a small space used for cooking food, a gallery, and a toilet. Each family made their space suitable for them.

When God wants to bless, He does it with generosity. The houses in the Hope village of Croix-des-Bouquets, compared to the houses of other villages built for people as badly affected as we were, had a much higher standard of space, equipment, and distribution. It was a real accompaniment from beginning to end where people have been duly relocated. It may not be the ideal house someone would have dreamed of if she/he had the means to build his/her own roof, but keep in mind we spent the first nights under the stars in the elements, which was uncomfortable especially during the early morning hours (2–3:00 a.m.). Living in tents for months and finally to end in a house rather decent like those of the village can only lead to gratitude.

The Advantages Offered by the Village

More Space

The dimension of space and environment play an important role in allowing reflection, planning, and vision for the future. After the months spent at the camp, my wife and I were advised by a couple, very respected for their faith and their love, to leave Canapé-Vert camp. We were reluctant because we understood that to separate from them would be disloyal after having experienced this whole tragedy with the group. When they saw our hesitation, they made it clear that if we stayed in the camp, it would be harder for us to have positive thoughts and make good decisions about the future of the church. "It may seem more difficult now to disconnect emotionally with them from the camp, but it is better to do so for the benefit of the group in the future," we were advised. This explanation led us to change our minds and to move.

So the more one is able to evolve in a reasonably spacious and less noisy environment, the more one is mentally prepared to perform better. At this level, the village with its 11,561 square meters more than the camp of the Canapé-Vert definitively offered to its occupants a better possibility of flourishing. Considering this, I have sometimes had the opportunity to be with young people in soccer matches, to ride a bicycle, or to do any sporting activity on the playing field. These activities greatly contribute to their mental, psychological, and physical development.

Better Human Relationships

Another reflection concerns the aspect of human relationships. The higher the level of heterogeneity in a given population, the more likely the possibility of conflict. Thus, we can argue that because the camp had a mostly homogenous population, conflict became less likely. The atmosphere was more calm and serene and therefore more livable.

An Improved Lifestyle

One of the great benefits is the possibility of having one's privacy — for example, the freedom for each family to decide what needs to be prepared for the meal. The menu was no longer imposed, and the brothers were no longer able to hear the sound of a voice crying through the camp: *"Attention, attention: food is ready!"* This "announcer" did his job well to the point that he had become the official deliverer of the messages to the campers. As soon as we heard his voice, we knew that we should prepare to get in the line toward the kitchen when our tent number was called. If for any reason we should be absent on this important call, someone else would be asked to remove a dish for you.

From a health point of view, too, the situation was no longer the same. There was no need to get in line for the restrooms during peak hours. Now, instead of having only two toilets that serve everyone, a total of forty-four private toilets were now available in the village, one per residence. What a big difference!

GRAPH OF COMPARISON					
	Accommodation Camp		*Village*		
	← →		← →		
Type of shelter		☐ *Tents*		☐ *Houses*	
Surface area	1339 m²	3–12m²	12.900m²	52m²	
Life time	Short, temporary	Short/ temporary	Long, lasting	Long/ lasting	
Life style	Community		Interdependent		
Sanitaires facilities	2 toilets	0	44 toilets and more	1 toilet	

If someone were to visit the village for the first time, without experiencing living in tents or living this experience personally or through someone else, it may not like seem like a huge difference between the two ways of life. However, here is what one of the beneficiaries of the village project reported after the camp experience at Canape-Vert:

I am Jean Lenet Charles, married and father of three children. I had the privilege of becoming a disciple of Jesus in March 2003. Since then, God has never ceased to do extraordinary things in my family's life. But nothing can inspire me more than what happened in my life during the event of January 12, 2010. I had barely got home with the joy of finding the family after a day of work. A few minutes later a strange noise broke out, and I soon realized it was an earthquake. All of a sudden the whole area was covered with ashes and dust. There were many shouts outside, and the people were running in all directions. Everything was dark, and it was believed that it was the apocalypse. Every minute that passed, we wondered how the next few days would unfold.

Two days later, I learned that an accommodation center had been initiated on the church property by the leaders to greet the disciples and their parents, victims of the catastrophe. That is how my family and I went to the church's room at the Canapé-Vert. And it was the dawn of a new life for us. We slept together and ate together thanks to the dedication of the leaders and the support of the sister churches through Hope Worldwide and Hope Worldwide-Haiti. Throughout this period, many young people have benefited from vocational training. Personally, I had the chance to complete my graduate studies. And in addition to multiple days of free consultation and vocational training, a large village was built to accommodate displaced families. Many families have benefited from houses built according to para-seismic standards. And my family is counted in this number. They are also supplied with drinking water and other infrastructure essential for the proper functioning of a human being. It was extraordinary grace. Many obstacles have been overcome, but life has resumed its rights in our church and in our families.

My family and I are truly grateful to our God who used brothers and sisters everywhere to give us a hand. We are happy to tell you that these materials have really helped to rebuild our lives and build a better tomorrow for our children. From the bottom of my heart, I thank you.

And to God be glory!

A better house and a better city.

The House

The process of transition into a home puts into perspective the promises of God about our celestial relocation. We had gone from a temporary tent in the accommodation camp to a more sustainable house in the village which structurally was more adequate. The same thing will happen from the spiritual point of view. The word of God is as follows:

> Do not let your hearts be troubled. You believe in God; believe also in me. My Father's house has many rooms; if that were not so, would I have told you that I am going there to prepare a place for you? And if I go and prepare a place for you, I will come back and take you to be with me that you also may be where I am. (John 14:1–3)

This promise is from Jesus Himself who gives us the guarantee that He has gone to prepare us a place. It is something to think about: the beauty of the abode that is reserved for us and the greatness of the city of God.

I used to read residential meters before being promoted to the category of industrial meter reader in this company that I had started in 1987. My job was to go from house to house to take the meter reading. So I can testify that there are some beautiful houses on earth. Go to Laboule or Belvil, Boutilliers or Montagne Noire and see how beautiful the residences of those areas are. They are real castles, some larger and more beautiful than others.

None of those houses, however, can be compared with a house in heaven.

The City

Many corners are extremely beautiful on the globe. One of them is probably on the north coast of Haiti. It is recognized among the most charming tourist sites of the island Hispaniola: Labadee. Despite all the problems facing the country of Haiti, Labadee is completely held out of turbulence of all kinds. It is a highly secure area, since it welcomes thousands of tourists on average every month.

The second and last time I had the chance to visit Labadee dates back to 1999. Already at that time, even before it became this gigantic resort, it had been a destination, put on the map of international tourism, and had severely restricted access to the site. And all the additional investments made since then have made Labadee even more attractive. The sea is of an azure blue, and the sand is fine and white. The whole area is planted in a natural setting, where the wild rocks (roches sauvages) mix. In 2009, the company that operates it had made significant disbursements of $55 million in order to make this tourist area a dream place. Today Labadee is barricaded and becomes like an island completely detached from the rest of the country. That's why when cruise ships land in the port of Labadee, the cruise passengers may not know they are in Haiti if they are not informed. Any Haitian cannot on a good morning decide he will visit Labadee. He will not be able to cross the barrier unless he has special permission from the management staff. Restriction has become even tighter than it was fifteen years ago, and there are more measures to protect space and maintain its standard of cleanliness.

Thus, in the musical repertory of the Tropicana orchestra, a group based in the city of Cap Haitian, we find this chorus which was integrated in one of its songs of the 1990s to enhance its brilliance: "*Labadee se paradi*" which means "Labadee is a paradise."

And for the heavenly city, what does the Bible tell us?

> The city was laid out like a square, as long as it was wide. He measured the city with the rod and found it to be 12,000 stadia in length, and as wide and high as it is long. The angel measured the wall using human measurement, and it was 144 cubits thick. The wall was made of jasper, and the city of pure gold, as pure as glass. The foundations of the city walls were decorated with every kind of precious stone. The first foundation was jasper, the second sapphire, the third agate, the fourth emerald, the fifth onyx, the sixth ruby, the seventh chrysolite, the eighth beryl, the ninth topaz, the tenth turquoise, the eleventh jacinth, and the twelfth amethyst. The twelve gates were twelve pearls, each gate made of a single pearl. The great street of the city was of gold, as pure as transparent glass. (Revelation 21:16–21)

I had the opportunity some time ago to visit a store where jewelry is sold. It seemed to me that he had barely opened his doors. In a promotional campaign, advertisements were used to invite the mall passersby to take a look. I was impressed by the way the window dressers put jewelry in the windows to capture the attention of customers. It was high-end jewelry: diamonds, gold, and other precious stones. They were sparkling because a system of lighting with special effects was installed there in order to radiate the store area, the windows, and especially the jewels.

So if a store of a few square meters can be so attractive just because of a few pieces that contain miniature gemstones, placed under the effect of special lighting in the windows, in addition to the low sweet classic music playing out of speakers camouflaged in the store's wall decoration, then what about the Holy City? Have you ever taken the time to imagine a great city built of pure gold, a city whose wall is built with a red gem called jasper and a city whose foundations of the walls are adorned with twelve precious stones? Each stone had a characteristic color. The emerald is of an intense green, the sardonyx of a brown red, and the chrysolite of a golden yellow, to mention only a few. Imagine all these precious stones of the wall incorporated into the city in pure gold. How much do you think this city will sparkle when the presence of God will project His light on the whole city? *Wow*! Have you ever cast a glance of this in your imagination? It will definitely be beautiful and extraordinary. Only the divine creator is capable of inventing such a setting for the city that will serve us as a dwelling place for all eternity.

Conditions of Access

When the decision to build the village of Croix-des-Bouquets had been stopped by the staff of the church in concert with Hope, the first step was to meet the potential candidates for the project to explain what was being planned to help them break the deadlock. After the acquisition of the land, they even went to make a prospective visit and to help with the work of barricading the property. From then on, they had begun to dream. The management of Hope Haiti had, on the same occasion, organized a series of meetings on a regular basis with interested parties of the project with the aim of keeping the prospective villagers informed and working with them on the conditions they should fulfill in order to be admitted to the project. It was not after the relocation that the conditions were given but long before, so the interested people could prove that they really wanted this change of housing by fulfilling the required formalities. If we humans know how to establish criteria that should lead to an impartial selection of those who must be admitted to our various programs, is it not just that God also gives us conditions leading us to the Holy City?

Now it is up to us to decide if we ever want to be taken with Jesus so that we are where He will be in the Father's house and so fulfill the requirements of the Bible: those of being clothed and not naked spiritually (2 Corinthians 5:3).

Benefits:

> I saw the Holy City, the New Jerusalem, coming down out of heaven from God, prepared as a bride beautifully dressed for her husband. And I heard a loud voice from the throne saying, "Look! God's dwelling place is now among the people and he will dwell with them. They will be his people, and God himself will be with them and be their God. 'He will wipe every tear from their eyes. There will be no more death[1] or mourning or crying or pain, for the old order of things has passed away." (Revelation 21:2–4)

Life on earth is the exact macro representation of what we experienced while living in the camp of Canapé-Vert. It is the tent that suffocated us during the day with the burning heat it released under the tropical sun. But, it is also that same tent that protected us during the rainy season and from the cold of the night. It is the long queue that caused our sweat when there was an emergency in the dwelling. However, it is also the sense of solidarity that motivated some to give up their turn for the benefit of the most vulnerable. It was a mixture of it all. And no one could solely enjoy its advantages without experiencing the inconveniences. This means that along with all the good things that life offers us; difficulties also infiltrate and place themselves on the other side of the scale, such that the existence itself has become this mixture of good and hard times.

However, when the saints will be relocated to this place reserved for us by Jesus, then we will have rest in the face of the sorrows and frustrations we have endured throughout our earthly pilgrimage. We will finally be able to participate in the Divine Glory forever.

Let us conclude this chapter of the relocation with a passage in which the apostle Paul expresses himself on the transition:

> For we know that if the earthly tent we live in is destroyed, we have a building from God, an eternal house in heaven, not built by human hands. Meanwhile we groan, longing to be clothed instead with our heavenly dwelling, because when we are clothed, we will not be found naked. (2 Corinthians 5:1–3)

The campers left the Canapé-Vert camp on Friday, September 23, 2011, after 619 days of encampment, to take possession of the village that was prepared for them.

I know that a day will come when the same will happen to the Christians. We will be taken to heaven to clothe ourselves in our heavenly home. The date is unknown, but we know that this spiritual relocation is certain. So, let's get ready!

CHAPTER 6

SURER WEALTH

SURER WEALTH

According to a document prepared by the government of the Republic of Haiti with the support of the international community (ht.undp.org), the total losses caused by the 2010 earthquake would be estimated at $7, 804 billion. This value in many aspects represents a good part of the wealth of Haiti acquired during the two centuries of its independence. It includes all buildings, roads, bridges, telephone systems, electricity, the distribution of water in homes, and rolling stock. It takes a lot in terms of time, financial resources, and skills to build the country and keep it running. And yet, how long did it take to change everything? Just a mere thirty-five seconds. The same observation is observed on the individual level. People have just seen the disappearance of their trade or small industry that they have acquired over the years at the cost of enormous sacrifices and hard labor. It is really disappointing to realize that it usually takes only a few minutes for what took us years to build to be destroyed. It is the evidence that nothing is sure and definitive here.

In his sermon on the mountain, Jesus told us,

"Do not store up for yourselves treasures on earth, where moths and vermin destroy, and where thieves break in and steal. But

store up for yourselves treasures in heaven, where moths and vermin do not destroy, and where thieves do not break in and steal. For where your treasure is, there your heart will be also . . ." (Matthew 6:19–21)

This recommendation of Jesus takes the opposite of our materialism. The great lesson that is conveyed in this passage is that even though these earthly treasures are necessary in response to our material needs, we must not allow them to become the main reason for our lives. According to a study, on a list of ten things by which man is constantly tempted, materialism occupies the top position.

In his book "King Jesus," Dr. Steve Kinnard explained it well when he said, "Possessions in themselves are not evil, but when we become greedy of our possessions, then we sin."[17]

Jaquot once had the privilege of meeting the most influential figure in town, Kortley Jirds. The latter decided to take a part of his inheritance to help a person every quarter to get out of poverty. The one who would first meet him on his way out of the chapel this morning came unannounced. At the time that the benefactor granted Jacquot to hear his request for breakfast, the opportunist explained in detail his problems. And at the end of the conversation, the rich man asked, "What can I offer you to get you out of misery?" After Jacquot had done some calculations using his calculator, followed by a few minutes of reflection, he answered that 30,000 Euros would be the reasonable amount that would get him out of financial embarrassment. "Are you sure my friend?" replied the rich man.

"Yes, without a doubt," assured the other. So, Kortley signed a check for the requested value. On returning home, after Jacquot had liquidated his debts with a portion of the money, he set up, with the rest, a small company that made him the new boss of the city. At the end of the story we find a prosperous Jacquot who actually came out of poverty. But, do you know that despite his success, Jacquot had a great regret? He said to himself:

"If I ever knew that he was so generous . . .

If only I knew . . . if . . .

He had asked me, if I was sure.

The mistake was mine.

My answer was yes.'

I leave you to imagine the rest. But, as indecent as it may seem, he carried this regret to the grave, trying in vain to meet again his benefactor around the chapel area.

This is the broken record of our dissatisfied hearts that always replays: "Much more, much more . . ."

Driven by our insecurity for the next day, we are continually tempted to take over all that is on our path.

Dany Laferrière in his book "**Tout bourge autour de moi**" traduced by "**Everything moves around me**" expresses a thought that applies well to this idea, when he writes:

"The enemy is not time, but all those things that have accumulated over the course of time. As soon as you pick up one thing, you cannot stop, for everything calls for another." [18]

This is where we must be careful not to fall into the trap of pursuing goods without restraint, especially if it is our relationship with God or our family that serves as burnt offerings on the altar of these acquisitions. We can have both a very decent but simple standard of living.

Do not wear yourself out to get rich; do not trust your own cleverness (Proverbs 23:4).

The disappointment of cooperatives

There was a serious financial crisis in 2002 related to the collapse of the cooperative system in Haiti. A cooperative is a financial institution that operates at a certain level like a bank. It receives the money from the depositors, makes it grow and gives its patrons in return a monthly interest fixed at a certain rate at the time of signing the contract. But at another level, it differs from the bank in that the depositors are the owners of the cooperative, while the bank is a public limited company. The other difference between these two entities lies in their management system. There was the time when the cooperatives budded like mushrooms in all the corners of the capital. Many Haitians, who believed in the cooperative movement, put large sums of money at the famous rate of 10% per month. In fact, it worked very well in the beginning to the point of becoming a national fever. Attracted by this bait for rapid capital growth, people who were already in the system were still looking to invest more money to have more profits. Some of the middle class, most reluctant or incapable, charmed by the testimony of friends and relatives, finally, after much hesitation decided to make huge sacrifices to invest at the cooperative. They even sold or used their mortgages of their only property or those funds for family emergency situations in order to register. It was a really contagious movement. And then what happened? Plop, the system collapsed, and depositors lost their assets. Can you imagine that? It was a disaster, a fatal blow for Haitian families. Not only because of the loss of their money, but also because it was their hope that had disappeared with the collapse of the cooperatives. The old Haitian proverb tells us: "Yo tap chache kout men, yo pran kout pie"; they were looking for betterment, and have given rise to decay.

So, there are many examples that clearly show that we cannot place our hope in our different systems—as credible as they appear—because of their fallibility. We cannot place our trust in our earthly treasures because of the ringworm, the rust, and thieves. Nothing is safe and definitive here.

What is the balance between greed and the pursuit of what is necessary for our needs?

According to the Universal Declaration of Human Rights (Article 25),

"Everyone shall have the right to a standard of living adequate for the health and well-being of himself and of his family, including food, clothing, Housing, medical care and necessary social services."

This article enumerates a list of reasonable things that could allow an individual to maintain the balance between extravagance and deprivation.

Solomon writes, *Give me neither poverty nor riches, but give me only my daily bread. Otherwise, I may have too much and disown you and say, 'Who is the Lord?' Or I may become poor and steal, and so dishonor the name of my God* (Proverbs 30:8–9).

A Christian should just fight and pray to have the necessities described in the list above to live decently and take care of the family. The Bible goes so far as to say *If we have food and clothing that will be enough* (1 Timothy 6:8).

Without advocating poverty, it is the idea of maintaining a simple standard of living without being caught in the trap of the seduction of wealth that tends to stifle the Word of God in our lives and render it fruitless (Matthew 13:22).

What would be the best things to pursue?

Invest for eternity!

A- Take care of the poor

For some time, technology has facilitated the transfer of funds globally. From one country to another or from one account to another, it is possible to realize large transactions at a distance in real time. For example, the region of East Asia and the Pacific was the first recipient of remittances in the world in 2015 with an amount of $127 billion. Much of this money was commercial and the other part was sent to families by the Diaspora. So in the modern world where we operate today, unless there is a special situation, transactions are no longer with the circulation of large volumes of money paper. Everything is settled electronically among financial institutions through the use of technology and accounting tools.

Another great thing to mention is that the diaspora also have the possibility to feed their bank accounts far in preparation of their retirement in their country of origin. They can make direct deposit into their account. So when the fateful time comes to return to their homeland, they can do it without worry because they had previously transferred the necessary resources they would need to live post-retirement.

In this sense, technology becomes a powerful weapon that makes everything easier. However, despite its efficiency, it is unable to help us transfer some of our earthly wealth to heaven.

Our currencies such as the dollar, the euro, the gourde and the yen are all completely incompatible with the celestial bank system. Now, if we want to make us treasures in heaven we must think of following the advice of Jesus to the rich young man.

"One thing you lack," he said. *"Go, sell everything you have and give to the poor, and you will have treasure in heaven. Then come, follow me"* (Mark 10:21).

As Christians, when we have made the decision to bow to God's demands to receive his grace, we are no longer of this world, even though we still live in it. We are only passing through the earth on our way to our final home, the Paradise. Now, if this is where we are meant to rest from our work, we should think about investing to increase our accounts there. Taking care of the poor is a way to forge a treasure in heaven and to convert our earthly treasures into heavenly treasures that cannot be destroyed by moth, rust, or thieves.

I can never be grateful enough for the work of HOPE WORLDWIDE throughout the world. Before the tragedy, the credit that I gave to this organization was coming from the fact that it is the legitimate daughter of our church's family. But, for now, my appreciation for Hope is based on what I saw on the ground during the earthquake. Haiti is definitely a good example where people's lives have been markedly improved during and after the hard time. It is a great inheritance that God gives us through His Kingdom. Every Christian should always carry Hope Worldwide in her heart and in her prayers, but also contribute so that it can continue to go where we cannot physically answer, when needs call us out. From one stone, two birds, the lives of people will be touched on the other side of the planet, and our celestial account will also grow.

B- Make Disciples

It is clear in the Bible that nothing can cross the threshold of the Holy City. Our material or immaterial goods are all limited to the land. Speaking to Timothy, Paul says, *"For we brought nothing into the world, and we can take nothing out of it"* (1 Timothy 6:7).

On the other hand, the Bible also said, *Do not be overawed when others grow rich, when the splendor of their houses increases they will take nothing with them when they die, their splendor will not descend with them* (Psalm 49:16–17).

You and I cannot do anything to change this rule. Yet God has given us a mission to seek souls lost to him during our pilgrimage. 2014 was a good year for me in terms of mission. With the Lord's help, I had the privilege to bear some personal fruits before leaving Haiti. When we arrived in Boston, seeing that 2015 had gone by without helping anyone to come to Christ despite our efforts, we soon realized that it would take much more faith to help others know God. I then began to pray with Junie for God to send us people who are open like the Ethiopian eunuch in Acts 8. One day in August 2016, I received a call asking me to meet a married couple, Al and Sandy. Our prayer was answered. Two months later, they made Jesus their Lord. Some other brothers and sisters were also involved. What refreshing it is! I say thank you to God for allowing us to be helpful in their conversion. We are truly encouraged by their faith.

To God is the glory!

I have found that there are places where making disciples is more complicated than others. Some brothers and sisters do not have the privilege to share their faith openly. In their booklet, *"Passport to the Land of Enough"* written by both

Dave Eastman and Joel Nagel, the first one did a vibrant testimony on the disciples' life in one of the European nations in these words:

"Disciples exercise prudent caution when sharing their faith, taking time to build relationships and establish trust; even then, they face rejection much more often than not. Three of the women I interviewed had been beaten because of their faith. All disciples are mocked. And though strong leaders have diligently worked the fields here, the church struggles to grow." [19]

It is clear that the challenges are not the same everywhere. For example, in the third world countries like Haiti, the socio-economic environment could be a serious handicap for a great number of people to come to Christ, especially when their sources of survival are challenged by God's word. On the other side, for the industrialized countries like the USA, people are rather distracted by the pressure that they are dealing with or by the opportunities that are pouring. And, for some other areas, the challenges are mostly due to religious and culture traditions. I am referring to certain countries of Asia and the Middle East.

But, regardless of the size and the nature of the challenge that preaching the gospel faces, the obstacle can always be moved by God. So, let's pray and have concrete deeds that show our true desire to give a chance to the lost world. And the Lord will be with us daily until the end of the world according to his promise.

Why is this so important?

This is very important because by opening our eyes to the other side, our material and intellectual goods will not follow us. Even small precious treasures that are portable will not cross the gate. It is not like here, where sometimes privileges are granted to someone through the authority of a parent or friend well positioned with power. Nor, is it a service we can buy because we have the means to pay for it. No one will be able to send a note, or make a phone call to ask for a hand to help us to cross with our much appreciated little treasures. For anything of earthly origin shall not enter into the house of God. But, by working in the field of God, the fruit which we have gathered for him, and which would have remained, is the only thing that can be converted into spiritual currency, which we shall have the possibility of having with us in the Holy City. All those souls who we fought for to be part of the cherished list of saints is what we can bring with us to heaven. It's so worth it.

Below is an excerpt from the article titled: **The Last Will of Alexander the Great,**

"The Emperor Alexander was ill and knew of his approaching death. He summoned his generals and communicated to them his last demands:

1. The best doctors should carry his coffin

2. The wealth he has accumulated (money, gold, precious stones) should be scattered along the procession to the cemetery, and

3. His hands should be let loose, hanging outside the coffin for all to see.

One of his generals who was surprised by these unusual requests asked Alexander to explain.

Here is what Alexander the Great had to say:

1. I want the best doctors to carry my coffin to demonstrate that, in the face of death, even the best doctors in the world have no power to heal

2. I want the road to be covered with my treasure so that everybody sees that material wealth acquired on earth, stays on earth

3. I want my hands to swing in the wind, so that people understand that we come to this world empty handed and we leave this world empty handed after the most precious treasure of all is exhausted, and that is TIME.

TIME is our most precious treasure because it is LIMITED. We can produce more wealth, but we cannot produce more time. When we give someone our time, we actually give a portion of our life that we will never take back. Our time is our life.

The best gift anyone can give is his time. ALWAYS give it to those you love." [20]

Conclusion

I believe that the reflections made by Alexander the Great at his deathbed should be considered by each individual. He invites us to see life with realistic eyes and an intelligent heart to understand that we have no guarantee here below. A day will come when we will be separated from what we are socially or have materially. Therefore, we are suggested by the Lord not to put our hope in the treasures on earth. Therefore, while cultivating a simple lifestyle, let's make investments that will bring fruit for eternity.

Let us remember the poor and seek souls lost to Christ. Because when we do this, we will find real treasures.

CHAPTER 7

LIFE GOES ON

LIFE GOES ON

"If you cannot fly, then run. If you cannot run, then walk. If you cannot walk, then crawl, but whatever you do, you have to keep moving" (Martin Luther King).

After the disaster of January 2010 in Haiti, many Haitians found themselves in the category of men and women of the world who carry deep wounds in their hearts to the memory of loved ones who were left in painful circumstances. Some have had the ability to recover more quickly. But for others, the gap is so deep that it is harder for them to find the formula that would allow them to get out of the emotional hole from where they felt. The belt that should provide them with a smooth transition from what they have experienced as trials to what they can still hope for seems to be unfit to bind these two realities together. It is the case of those who are in continual depression, without having the strength to rise again. It is also the case of those who are so weak at the point in time to think about suicide. Allow me to offer you the following lines people who know difficult situations like you and who can encourage you by their story.

1) A human model in the past

Have you ever heard of Martin Gray? I had the opportunity to read a few books from this author's collection several years ago. And nothing can be more inspiring than to see someone show such tenacity during his 93 years of life. The last time I tasted one of his last works of the time, dates back to 1980–81. I was a teenager. And I am always inhabited during all these years by the image of this man of courage that I met through his works. Martin Gray lost his entire family twice. The first time he was hit dates back to World War II (1939–1945), when his two parents and two brothers were killed by the deadly Nazi machine in Poland. He was then a young teenager of 17 years and destroyed emotionally.

But he still managed to find a way to make his way. And the second time, it was a forest fire that killed his wife and four children in the South-East of France. And he alone survived these painful events to become an emblematic figure of strength and desire to continue despite everything. A 20th century model of courage for all those who have witnessed difficult times just like him.

In one of his books, "**The Book of Life**," he writes:

"To be faithful to those who have died is not to shut oneself in his grief. It is necessary to continue to dig one's path: straight ahead as they would have done it themselves. As we would have done it with them. For them. To be faithful to those who are dead is to live as they would have lived. And make them live in us. And bequeath their face, their voice, their message to others."

Martin Gray could easily have been won over by depression and excessive discouragement that have so often tangled his entrails. He could have just left a dark note that he would attach to a place that everyone would see at first glance, with the words *"I cracked under the weight of my grief, Farewell."* Of course, it would have thrown the public's attention, but it would have been done. However, instead of pitying one's fate, and leaving a note of sadness, one sees it rather to opt—after having lived through one's bereavement—to contaminate others by his determination not to stop, through all the notes of which his books are scattered. We all sometimes need to find, in the example of another, the vitamin of the moral force we lack to get rid of the glue of discouragement and pessimism that we hold for too long, clinging to our misfortunes of the past without the wounds they produce are never cicatrized.

If this can help you, start thinking about this promise of God where it is mentioned.

"For I know the plans I have for you," declares the LORD, "plans to prosper you and not to harm you, plans to give you hope and a future." (Jeremiah 29:11)

2) A human model in a recent time

I would like to introduce someone who has had great struggles in his life in recent years and it is he who will directly share his story with you:

"My name is Jassaint Denis and I am glad to be able, through my humble sharing, to add a note of encouragement to this chapter of the book dedicated to those who like me lost, at least, a loved one during the earthquake of January 12, 2010 in Haiti.

To begin with, I would simply say it was a huge loss to me, given what this person represented in my life. Rose, of her full name, was not only a wife, but above all a sister and a good friend to me.

Forgive me for not detailing the romantic beginnings of our love story. But, of a good friendship, we had become two lovers who

145

went out together. Of two lovers, we have passed the betrothal stage, to become a married couple and solid with the help of God. And it was from this couple that Jassainah our pretty little girl was born. I believe that for the time we had lived together, it was a great blessing until the drama came.

How did I experience the event?

Usually, our couple's schedule was as follows: we left the house together in the morning to each go to our respective office. I dropped her first and then I continued to my work, then to the university. And in the afternoon I went to get her to go back to our home. So this afternoon when the earth began to vibrate, I was passing a test on the seventh floor of the building that houses my school. Suddenly, the furniture and the students were tossed about by the force of the jolt. Shouts were heard from all over the university. And in my astonishment, I remember saying this: Lord, I am not ready to die now.

When the great shock ceased, I tried as well as everyone else to look for the members of my family, looking for Rose first. As I was still far from her office, I could not imagine that what I saw remotely was real: the 4-storey building that housed Rose's office had fallen flat with her in its stomach.

At that point, all the strength that animated me at that precise moment had left me. The shock was so brutal that I could not even stand on my legs. I had to kneel to let go the cries of my torn heart. All of a sudden everything had melted like butter placed in a pan heated to white: our plans, our dreams, our friendship, and our love. Everything had become so disturbing and melancholy that I almost lost my head.

But unfortunately! I had to face it.

I believe I experienced the loss of Rose in three stages:

Confusion

During the first five days after the earthquake, I was very confused. Despite the research done by the mechanical pearls, the body of my wife had not yet been discovered. I thought during the excavations, that maybe she had to retire before the drama. I was trying to forge a reason to hope that Rose would come back soon. At least it was my dearest wish in my sub consciousness.

Acceptance

When we finally discovered the body already in putrefaction after five days, it is then that for me began the stage of acceptance that Rose is indeed dead. And she will not come back. It was really over.

Managing this new reality

Here I am suddenly struggling with a reality for which I was not mentally prepared. A nine month old girl in my arms without her mother. It was the stage where life seemed unbearable to me. My troubles, my anguish, my rebellions, and my desire to abandon everything.

It is at this lowest crossroads of my whole existence, disoriented, and that for four years and a few months until God sends a ray of sunshine in my life, thus ending this journey that is difficult to digest. Another friend, another sister, another mother for Sassoue and another wife for me.

Scripture tells us:

I lift up my eyes to the mountains where does my help come from? My help comes from the LORD, the Maker of heaven and earth (Psalm 121:1–2).

I first say a big thank you to the Lord who helped me to recover myself. But a big thank you also goes to Viviane for accepting to open this new page in my life and that of Sassoue. I am very grateful to you my dear.

> *To all those who are still struggling to get up, I would encourage them to trust the Lord. He is a God capable of filling the void that others have left in our lives. I am not saying that He will necessarily send someone into your lives following the same pattern in my case. But God is great, and has so many solutions, that he will do for you what will best suit your emotional, material and spiritual needs."* End of the story.

3) A biblical model

It is true that other people who have experienced difficult situations like ours can reach out to us, but there is no one who can better sympathize with us than God in times of weaknesses.

1 Corinthians 10:13, we read this, *No temptation has overtaken you except what is common to mankind. **And God is faithful; he will not let you be tempted beyond what you can bear . . .***

All temptations have their size and striking force. But they can never come to us without being weighed and permitted by God according to our ability to manage them.

The case of Prophet Elijah

While he himself went a day's journey into the wilderness. He came to a broom bush, sat down under it and prayed that he might die. "I have had enough, LORD," he said. "Take my life; I am no better than my ancestors. Then he lay down under the bush and fell asleep.

All at once an angel touched him and said, "Get up and eat." He looked around, and there by his head was some bread baked over hot coals, and a jar of water. He ate and drank and then lay down again.

The angel of the LORD came back a second time and touched him and said, "Get up and eat, for the journey is too much for you." So he got up and ate and drank. Strengthened by that food, he traveled forty days and forty nights until he reached Horeb, the mountain of God. (1 Kings 19:4–8)

All temptations have their size and striking force. But they can never come to us without being weighed and permitted by God according to our ability to manage them.

This passage is about the prophet Elijah. He was very discouraged in his life to the point where he asked for death. And this happened right after his victory over the prophets of Baal, and that of God's response to his prayer for it to rain. So if a prophet of the caliber of Elijah, who accomplished so many great things for God, could feel so weak, you will agree with me that no one is exempt from discouragement. As strong or spiritual as one may be, one can also know in the desert, times of discouragement.

The partition of God in the recovery process of Elijah

The angel of the Lord twice gave him what he needed to recover. Elijah was so morally low that he needed a double portion of the same menu. But we see the patience of God manifested toward him by delegating his Angel the number of times that the situation of the servant required it until the force returned to him.

The partition of Elijah in the process of his own recovery

It is true that the angel brought him the cake and the jug of water, but it was not the Angel who had opened his mouth for him to taste the cake in small bites, nor to swallow the water by Small sips. On both occasions, it was up to Elijah to get up and eat. We do not know how long it took him to finish his portion, but at the end of the day, he had nothing left of what the Angel had brought him. It was beyond the power of his recovery.

The lesson we can learn from this story is that it will always take us an effort to get out of the hole of discouragement where we are held back now. It will not be up to you to find the ingredients to prepare the cake and find the source where the water should be drawn, but it is your responsibility to stand up, eat and drink.

Two things would be suggested

I. Rejuvenate first in the word of God.

For it is said: *Come to me, all you who are weary and burdened, and I will give you rest. Take my yoke upon you and learn from me, for I am gentle and humble in heart, and you will find rest for your souls.* (Matthew 11:28–29)

Take God at his Word.
Please refer to the chapter
"Solid without cement" and
see what is suggested to
those who are drowning.

II. Why not consult a
professional?

After the earthquake, there
are scenes that some of us

> It will always take us an effort to get out of the hole of discouragement where we are held back now. It will not be up to us to find neither the necessary ingredients to prepare the cake nor the source where the water should be drawn, but it will be our responsibility to stand up, eat and drink.

have experienced that require the intervention of professionals,
so strong was the shock. A team of psychologists worked with us
to help us manage this amount of stress that suddenly struck us.

Personally, I do not know how many times I started running
to protect myself by believing I felt an earthquake. But, when
everyone indiscriminately tells me that they did not feel it
themselves, then I finally understood that it was rather a tremor
that manifested itself in my head.

One Sunday I was preaching at the Cayes church, it was the
first time after the earthquake that I stayed high on a platform
for so long. I had the strange sensation that the building was
going to collapse, as soon as I glanced outside, however eva-
sive. I had learned to control myself, watching the others qui-
etly sitting. As soon as they had remained calm, I knew there
was nothing to fear.

Everything was fine in the end, but I had to fight with the reality
of being upstairs. Help, yes, we really needed it for a better
management of the after-effects of the trauma that inhabited
us for a long time after the disaster. So, a big thank you to this
team of foreign and local psychologists who put themselves
at our disposal at Canapé-Vert to support us during this time.

This can be helpful in other cases as well as yours. So, do not hesitate to try this approach.

Why should one make the effort to get up and eat?

Remember what Elijah asked the Lord at the beginning of history. Under the weight of discouragement he solicited death. And why do you think that instead of death, God sent him cake and water? Why, instead of a raven or another person like the lady of Sarepta used in other circumstances to serve the prophet, did God this time explicitly send his Angel to go to Elijah's side twice? Why should we ask?

The first answer is that at this critical point where Elijah was, God had to take a measure proportional to his situation to help him rebuild the slope by sending the Angel to him with what he needed. For this time, it was not a raven or any living being that would better meet his needs, but a specialist delegated in twice. God has always probed and weighed the depth and weight of our problems in order to put at our disposal what we really need to be restored from every point of view.

But, it is important to understand that all this change was possible in Elijah's life because he had left the door open for God to work. He was under great pressure to the point of opting for death in his agony, but was careful however not to touch his own life. And after that, we found him back on track.

The example of the prophet Elijah should motivate us to fight against discouragement, and to begin to dream again. God has many more things in store for us who are down.

The years after the earthquake were really grueling for Junie and me. With the help of the other staff members, we were able to help the church in the difficult time of the crisis. And,

I will not stop thanking God to have allowed us to serve his people during that time. But, months later, three members of the family got real sick, but functional. In addition to the challenges that were linked to the different aspects of the ministry in the post-crisis impasse that had literally swamped us, our faith had been sorely tested. Then, after seeking advice and praying, we made the decision to take a sabbatical in the ministry and seek medical treatment for the whole family, especially for one of our boys who had special needs. The point in the story is that although I was aware of the problems, I never thought of leaving the ministry, since that was my job, but also my passion. I really love to preach. And I like to study the Bible with people, and live the suspense of the process of change that God usually operates in their lives through His Word. However, when my wife honestly expressed her concerns, I had to reconsider everything and put priorities in their right order. It was a somewhat tense conversation because it caused us to reassess our leadership position at the church level, but also our future. I have been in the ministry for 20 years, which meant that the work in Haiti had become like a part of us. After that conversation, however, it was obvious that God wanted for us to take a break for the well-being of the family first, but the church as well. And from that moment, no need to say how many unanswered questions haunted us. It was our turn to take a dose of the medicine we often prescribed to the disciples in Haiti in difficult time, "**Trust God**." I thank the Lord for allowing us to be open with each other as a couple, to have been able to talk honestly about what caused fear and insecurity about tomorrow, and to want to face them together.

Today, we are far from the body of the ministry in Haiti for a time. It is true; we really missed our dear friends. They have always supported us all in good and bad times. We also missed the church scattered all over the country: Cap-Haitian, Cayes, Mirebalais, Bodarie, Irois, Jacmel, Carrefour, Clercine, Croix des Bouquets, especially the congregation in Port-au-Prince. But in the end, what can we conclude in the face of this reality that separates us? All the changes, even the most desired, have their melancholy (Anatole France). And unfortunately, we are not exempt in this rule. But, on the other hand, we read: *And we know that in all things God works for the good of those who love him* . . . (Romans 8:28)

To close this chapter, I would like to applaud the courage of the Church in Haiti. The year 2010 was indisputably the hardest year in the whole history of the church. Yes, we faced a lot, especially during the first weeks after the catastrophe: the wounded to care for, the displaced to house, the mourners to comfort. That was enough to bend the church, but, I saw it rise up to make a difference at that crossroad of big confusion. I remember this group of brothers who put their lives at risk under the aftershocks to relieve those who were stuck between the cement walls the day after January 12. At another level, I would have watched this vast movement of mobilization of the Christians to help more than one hundred people to come to Christ throughout the whole country in that same year of tribulation. What can I say? You are an extraordinary Church, a source of inspiration for all who visited you during that time.

When I think about the church in Haiti and the group of leaders who give their heart and soul for the work of the Lord, these words of the Apostle Paul come to mind.

Rather, as servants of God we commend ourselves in every way: in great endurance; in troubles, hardships and distresses . . . sorrowful, yet always rejoicing; poor, yet making many rich; having nothing, and yet possessing everything. (2 Corinthians 6:4–10)

Yes, you have always been this church before, during and after the tragedy. And my prayer is that your light continues to shine for the glory of God.

Finally, I would simply say that this God who took care of Elijah in the desert, who visited my family during the transition period, will also visit you in the wilderness of your life. This same faithful God who encircled the Church in Haiti during the earthquake crisis will also encircle you in the midst of your own earthquake. And this God, who sustained Jassaint by filling his life with grace, will also do what is necessary to provide a way out for you at the right time.

Why?

Because, as long as there is life, there will be hope with this same God who is also ours.

CHAPTER 8

THE GRATITUDE

THE GRATITUDE

This book would be incomplete if this chapter had not been integrated.

From that date January 13, 2010 until the relocation of the people who were part of the camp, many things have really changed in our lives. Progress was evident. In one of the antecedent chapters, I cited a number of actions that have contributed to our success: food for over a hundred people for several months, psychological and medical assistance, tents, vocational training, and the erection of the village to relocate people.

That was already a lot, not to mention the non-palpable things that we also benefited, such as phone calls, prayers, and the presence of many brothers and sisters who had come from far away to encourage us in this situation. The words would be missing, if we should mention all the details that marked us.

It is clear to us, the beneficiaries, that a lot of both financial and human resources had been mobilized to get us out of the impasse. Is this why this chapter is written, so that the voice of the church of Haiti may be heard in the distance?

Why?

Look at what the Bible says,

Now on his way to Jerusalem, Jesus traveled along the border between Samaria and Galilee. As he was going into a village, ten men who had leprosy met him. They stood at a distance and called out in a loud voice, "Jesus, Master, have pity on us!"

When he saw them, he said, "Go, show yourselves to the priests." And as they went, they were cleansed.

One of them, when he saw he was healed, came back, praising God in a loud voice. He threw himself at Jesus' feet and thanked him—and he was a Samaritan.

Jesus asked, "Were not all ten cleansed? Where are the other nine? Has no one returned to give praise to God except this foreigner?" Then he said to him, "Rise and go; your faith has made you well. (Luke 17:11–19)

The church of Haiti wanted to return to signify its gratitude to its benefactors. According to the figures given in this passage, only one person in ten would be grateful for the benefits received.

Jean Francois Marmontel rightly says,

"Nothing in the world is rarer than sincere gratitude, and nothing is more common than an odious ingratitude" (Leçons d'un père à ses enfants -1806).

This is something that everyone should look after because we live in a world that makes a clean sweep of recognition. Everything is taken for free, as if it were due. The children say they did not ask their parents to give them birth, and that it would be their duty to sacrifice themselves for them, without expecting anything in return. The members of the church think that the Pastor or the Evangelist is paid for his work, and all they have to do is give their contribution. In Third World countries, where people are able to employ small staff for their domestic tasks, the latter, instead of being respected and encouraged by Monsieur or Madame for the work they provide, are rather verbally maltreated to ensure that the distance of rank is well maintained between the boss and the servant. And what about the effort of the spouse who is often not appreciated enough by the other?

The deficiency of gratitude becomes a scourge that character-izes our society. Some have a great deal of hesitation in rec-ognizing what others have contributed to the record of honor. The parents loved us and raised us. The elders framed us. The teachers have taught us. And finally, the friends encouraged and advised us to go further. It is all these bricks placed side by side by these different actors that make us this important element of the social chain, of which we have become. No one can deny that he did not forge himself alone.

At this crossroads, it is important to cultivate recognition.

Why is the church in Haiti grateful?

We are grateful, because we realized that among all the victims that the earthquake left behind, we were among the best treated, if not the best treated. According to an article entitled, *"Three years after the earthquake, Haiti between camps and shanty-towns"* published by the Archipelago of Science on its web-site on January 11, 2013, the population of the victims would form about 496 camps in the aftermath of the earthquake[21]. And of all these camps, ours compared to them had been like an oasis in the middle of the desert. We did not suffer from hunger or thirst. We were among the first to be provided with equipment that protected us from the cold of the night and from the showers.

I remember one night around one o'clock, after we had received the tents, the torrential rain struck Port-au-Prince. And this rain buried the nail in the back of many of the victims, making their situation even more chaotic. Indeed, there was another camp lodging that was located in the public square of the Canapé-Vert, about 500 meters of ours. The noise that reached this late hour of the night was enormous. The people of the neighboring camp were in distress.

What was their situation? The majority of the occupants of this camp did not have good tents. Their tents had been forged with canvas by themselves, tents that could only protect them from the burning sun of the day, not against the rain. Their cry had broken my heart, thinking that if only this shower had occurred a few days earlier, we would be in the same situation as they. I was sober and grateful that these cries were not far from us, but not among us. I prayed to say thank you to God, but also to ask Him to have mercy on people who were not as well equipped as we were under such circumstances. I was thinking mainly of the children on the other side of the fence. While our men were asleep, they were under gutters. I believe that the feeling of gratitude that passed through me also con-taminated all the others of the camp of the church. When the morning awoke, this rain was at the heart of all speeches. For not only was it strong, but it was the first that had been received after the drama. On our side, we commented on the shouts we had heard in the evening, recognizing that God had done this to show us clearly that He was with us. Also, we were inclined to better appreciate what we had received so far. But as we turned around on the other side in the morning, talking to our neighbors, and looking at their installation, it was obvious to us that, despite the difficulties, we were a greatly blessed group.

Why are we grateful?

We are grateful for all the comfort visits we received. They had come from everywhere: the Dominican Republic, Canada, the US, and Europe. Many of the visitors would never have chosen Haiti as their destination because of the poor state of the country. However, their love led them to the lodging camp of the church at Canapé-Vert, braving all the risks, in order to see us, and touch us closely. One cannot imagine how refreshing these visits were.

I can still see Mollie Mostert, that sister who traveled from Los Angeles to gratify us with her presence. I would like to give her a symbolic medal of dean. For, of all the people who have visited us in the host camp, perhaps hundreds, Mollie was visibly the least young. What is most touching with her is the fact that despite her age, she had shown herself so young at heart, not to be intimidated by the duration of the flights that should lead her to us in Port-Au-Prince. And the time she spent with us is engraved in big letters in our memories. She spoke to the sisters, and on the eve of her return to Los Angeles, she organized a party for them as an encouragement. Then, after she left, she kept calling to maintain contact with us. These are gestures without prizes. Thank you very much Mollie for your spirit of sacrifice and love.

Why are we grateful?

We are grateful for the value of fraternal communion in our family of churches. The earthquake had carried Port-au-Prince airport infrastructure. As a result, commercial aircraft could not use them. So the link between Haiti and the rest of the world was virtually cut off by air. It is encouraging to see how the Church of Santo Domingo served as a relay in this situation between the international community and us at Canapé-Vert.

All the aid we received during the state of emergency were planned at the level of Santo Domingo and then transported by land, where our borders are common. Not only did they organize trips for those who were passing through their homes, sometimes accompanying them to Port-au-Prince, but they offered themselves, helping us in the medical field. We greatly appreciated this help.

And what about all the other churches that supported us in one way or another? I will never be able to finish the list of all those who have intervened in our favor. A special word goes to the place of The Church of Miami. It was she who allowed the members of the staff to withdraw a bit by paying a few days of vacation, after having worked hard to put off those who were in difficulty at the level of the congregation of Port-au-Prince. And how can we thank the New York City church of Christ? The Church of Haiti is more than a quarter of a century old, and New York has supported us all these years to a very large extent. The work that was carried out in Haiti until then is financially due to this congregation, which annually sends us an allowance to supplement our operating budget. In this respect I would like to say in a special way, on behalf of the Haitian church, a great THANK YOU to all the disciples of the New York City Church of Christ for never neglecting to give their money in the special contribution taken each year for missions. Know that your money given as a sacrifice to the Lord performs miracles on the island. Men and women are continually baptized after receiving the message of the gospel. Not only have we been supported in our operating budget, but in difficult times like the earthquake, the New York Church is still standing by our side.

Finally, I would like to mention the Church of Monrovia in Liberia. The Republic of Haiti is 6932 kilometers from this Republic which is located in West Africa. There was no contact with them before. But when the earthquake struck, this congregation found a way to contact us, and to send us some help in cash, accompanied by a note of encouragement. This gesture, because it comes from very far away, and from a Church with which we were not connected before, had really touched our hearts. The unity that God gives us through His Kingdom is an achievement that should not be exchanged for anything in the world. On the contrary, we need to do our best to improve it.

Why are we still grateful?

We are grateful for all our brothers and sisters from all over the world who have not hesitated to make a gesture during the gathering for Haiti in their congregation. They have given with good heart to people whom, perhaps, they will never meet here below, except in the day when we shall be reunited with our Lord Jesus. But know that—if the opportunity is not offered to you to undertake a trip to Haiti to see it with your own eyes— your offer made a big difference in our lives during the crisis.

Why are we grateful?

We are grateful for Hope Worldwide, and for Hope Worldwide Haiti. Our exit from the tunnel was the result of a good coordination between these two entities. The sense of good management has been honored. In a context where hundreds of non-governmental organizations (according to an article signed by Le Nouvelliste published on 02–02–11, there are 495 NGOs) registered as operating in Haiti in the aftermath of the earthquake to lend their support to the people. Obviously there was a lot of money raised for that purpose. From what we saw on the ground, we realized that it is not just having funds allocated to a rubric "*for Haitians affected by the earthquake of January 2010" that* improves the quality of people's lives. Definitely, this is not enough; otherwise, there would not be—eight years later—any people who would still be bent in makeshift tents in accommodation camps. But it is the money handled wisely by the managers that brings the hope wished for by donors as well as by the victims, as was the case for us in the camp of the Church at Canapé-Vert. In this sense, Hope has become a great blessing, not only for our churches, but also for all communities where their operations extend. Our thanks go to the staff of Hope Worldwide and Hope Worldwide Haiti for putting all their capacity in motion, in order to bring that hope that our situation required.

Hope (Single Corps) is helping to paint some houses in the village

I also cannot forget "Haitian Support," which has undertaken major actions at the Bodarie zone in the field of education to improve the lives of the children in this withdrawn area of Haiti. It is touching to see people coming from afar to Port-au-Prince, then to travel several tens of kilometers on a road rampant and rocky just to give of them, serving the deprived of this rural community. These are gestures for which we are infinitely grateful. On behalf of all the children of Bodarie, I say a big thanks to Haitian support.

Why are we grateful?

We are also grateful for the church in Charleston South Carolina that has for many years adopted the church in Mirebalais by developing a partnership with it. Because of that partnership, the brothers and sisters in Mirebalais are so encouraged by the love that they get from their sister church.

Why are we grateful?

Lastly, we are grateful for CHALÈ KRÉOL that allowed us to have our first meals at the beginning of the crisis.

Thank you so much.

The language of ingratitude and recognition

The ungrateful heart said, "It was not I who asked you to do this for me."

The grateful heart takes into consideration all that it receives.

The ungrateful heart, in comparing himself with those who have more than him, thinks he's punished.

The grateful heart, by comparing itself to the destitute, feels blessed.

The ungrateful heart quickly forgets a blessing and its author.

The grateful heart keeps the memory of a benefactor forever.

The ungrateful heart thinks of merit without any royalty.

The grateful heart is full of appreciation and remains far from indifference.

The thankfulness of the ungrateful heart comes from his lips.

The thankfulness of the grateful heart comes from its depth and without truce

Conclusion

Thank God you loved me! Oh thank God you blessed me. Thank God for your kindness. You loved my life.

I want to say thank you, you loved me. A thousand thanks you have saved my soul.

Reveal to me all your desires that I may serve you for eternity. May my life be your pleasure, fashioned as you please.

I want to say thank you, you loved me. A thousand thanks, you have saved my soul.

These are the words of a very familiar song that are used here to conclude this chapter. This canticle translates the exact expression of our hearts toward a God who has done so much for us.

Conclusion of the book

I would like to finish the book with the same idea that I introduced it. I said, speaking of the earthquake, "That it must also be perceived as a warning signal triggered by God to attract to Him our people's attention, in order to learn how to place our milestones on the right side."

Even though we, the survivors of the tragedy, were not all in the same city where the impact of the earthquake had been most felt, like: Jacmel, Léogâne or Port-au-Prince, even if we were in different activities like: work, school, behind the wheel, or in the streets, and even if we have lived it in a different way, nobody can pretend not to have been touched by the cataclysm.

But the question we must all ask ourselves is:

What did we learn?

1) For ourselves

I hope your investment has not been in vain. In my opinion, a book costs a lot. It takes money to have it and time to read it. In the end, you should get an idea of what really happened in Haiti. But also draw a lesson that is personal.

We do not all have the same situation at the time of reading this book, but we can all come up with strong resolutions that will influence positively our lives in the future. This is only possible if we understand the message that is communicated through the 2010 destructive earthquake in Haiti. The first thing to consider is our fragility. We are all vulnerable beings. What we are or have does not protect us from the diseases and the various accidents that occur. This leaves us with only one choice, to learn to navigate wisely.

It is time to think more than ever about our relationship with God. Time to stop giving ourselves to religious rituals, but to embrace spirituality.

Remember, it is by the faithfulness of God that we are kept alive. Let us seize the opportunity to do the necessary preparation until our time arrives.

So build on solid ground—the Word of God—to have the hope of the blessed Eternity that the Lord Jesus promised.

2) For the country afterwards

According to an article entitled "***Haiti as vulnerable in 2016 as in 2010,***" according to Claude Prépetit following an interview given by the latter to the newspaper "*Le National,*" on January 12, 2016, He made it known and I quote:

"Any other earthquake will be catastrophic. The country is more vulnerable than ever, says the geologist who pointed out that construction standards have not been met literally since after January 12, 2010 to date. Houses have been rebuilt without observing seismic standards. Some individuals have rehabilitated houses that deserve to be rebuilt in full. The competent authorities remain passive in this situation. This has, in one way or another, enabled the researcher to confirm a very high level of risk and vulnerability at the country level" (Lenational.org).

It is not this kind of diagnosis that I would wish to read or to hear in the media. This report reveals how quickly we forget, setting aside the lessons we are supposed to learn eight years later. According to the former French military commander speech, Ferdinand Jean Marie Foch, well known for his prowess during the First World War, he mentioned that a man without memory is a lifeless man, and people without memory are people without a future.

At this level, I think it is imperative to make the necessary correction so that the next book or film of our people's history will be better written for the next generation's benefit. So that we could finally stop saying: "*si nou t konen" paske, li toujou dèyè,* **that means, "If we knew" because, it always comes after.**

REFERENCES

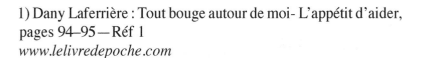

1) Dany Laferrière : Tout bouge autour de moi- L'appétit d'aider, pages 94–95 — Réf 1
www.lelivredepoche.com

2) Bilan- {Article 10512 : « *Haiti-Séisme / Un an, les chiffres clés de ces derniers 12 mois* »publié Le 11 Janvier 2011 par Alter presse} — Réf 2
www.alterpresse.org

3) Charles Nisard, histoire des livres populaires ou de la littérature du Colportage, 1864 — Réf 3
www.fr.m.wiktionary.org

4) Ing Claude Prépetit : « *Aléa et risque sismique en Haiti* » Réf 4
web.ics.purdue.edu

5) François Duvalier au pouvoir : de la répression politique à la disparition des espaces de libertés économique et culturelle. (1957–1971)
La Diaspora Haïtienne| Cédric Audebert. Presses Universitaires de Rennes. Réf 5
www.books.openedition.org|pur26973

6) Le Chili, une zone sismique à risques. Le Figaro.fr Publié le 27–02–2010 — Réf 6
www.lefigaro.fr
20 Janvier 2010

7) Les bâtiments détruits 20 Janvier 2010 « Haiti-Séisme I Un an, les chiffres clés de ces 12 Mois » publié le 11 janvier 2011. Réf 7
www.alterpresse.org

8) Guide de survie à Boston, après quelques tempêtes de neige. neige-hiver-Boston/ 11 Février 2015. Réf 8
www.maathiildee.com/

9) 20 Janvier 2010 — Un second tremblement de terre de 6.1 magnitude Richter.
Publié par aidonshaïti le 14I04I2010 — Réf 9
www.aidonshaïti.centerblog.net

10) Quantité estimative de déblais ramassée
« *Haïti- Séisme I Un an, les chiffres clés de ces 12 mois* » publié le 11 janvier 2011 — Réf 10
www.alterpresse.org

11) « *Une personne se suicide toutes les 40 secondes dans le monde* »
Le Monde.fr 04I09I2014 — Réf 11
www.mobile.lemonde.fr

12) Vie à Rome dans l'antiquité — Statistiques — Réf 12
www.causes-economique.com

13) Les sinistrés

« *Haïti—Séisme / Un an, les chiffres clés de ces 12 mois* » publié le 11 janvier 2011. Réf 13

www.alterpresse.org

14) Marek Halter: La violence commence où la parole s'arrête—Réf 14

www.evene.lefigaro.fr

15) Dwight Carlson, MD: Overcoming Hurts and Anger. Réf 15—Page 100.

ISBN: 9780736968331

www.HarvestHousePublishers.

16) Dwight Carlson, MD: Overcoming Hurts and Anger. Réf 16—Page 72.

ISBN: 9780736968331

www.HarvestHousePublishers

17) Dr G. Steve Kinnard: King Jesus, chapitre 9, Page 201

ISBN—13 978–1939086–57–0—Réf 17

www.ipibooks.com

18) Dany Laferrière: Tout bouge autour de moi- Les choses, page 19—Réf 18

www.lelivredepoche.com

19) Dave Eastman and Joel Nagel: Passport to the Land of Enough.

''Sunday Meditation Istanbul'' Page 31—Réf 19

www.GetGroundedForLife.com

20) Les dernières volontés d'Alexandre Le Grand—Réf 20

(*www.jkania.free.fr*)

21) Le nombre de camps
« *Haïti—Séisme /Un an, les chiffres clé de ces 12 mois* » publié
le 11 Janvier 2011—Réf 21
www.alterpresse.org

Note: The biblical references used in this book are all from the
NIV BIBLE version.

CPSIA information can be obtained
at www.ICGtesting.com
Printed in the USA
FSHW01n0106250418
47265FS

9 781545 626856